# THE

# MILLENNIAL

# TAKEOVER

By
**Kenneth Cheadle**

ISBN: 978-0-9983262-0-7

https://www.facebook.com/KennethCheadleCoach/

http://www.kennethcheadle.com

https://twitter.com/KennethCheadle

https://www.instagram.com/kennethcheadle/

# ACKNOWLEDGEMENTS

So many people and experiences have inspired this book that it would be impossible to mention them all. However, I would like to give special thanks to Michelle Richardson, TaQuisha Richardson, Tamica Richardson, Rosemary Wiggins, Marshall Richardson, Cassandra Richardson, Dr. Lawerence McNair, Sergeant Major Corey Jackson, The Deberry Twins, Lauren McGrail, Myron McCant, Richardson family, Cheadle family, Crew family, military family, consultant family, and to my wife, Carissa.

# TABLE OF CONTENTS

# INTRODUCTION

Ready or not, millennials will soon take over the previous generations as the leaders in corporate America. I wanted to help prepare them for that spot — for that takeover.

As a career coach, I have found fulfillment as I live out my why: helping people (more on what a 'why' is to come). It may sound cliché, but in all honesty, this book is strictly intended to help others achieve success.

As a first generation career professional in my family, part of my struggle was that I didn't have family members to help guide me. Initially, I thought I was the only one who felt like an imposter in corporate America. I grew up in the inner city, joined the military, and came from a poor family — and I didn't feel like I fit in at work. It wasn't easy.

However, I soon discovered I wasn't the only person who felt this way. There were others who had the desire to excel in their careers, but they didn't know how. They had the desire, but not the road map. They had the vehicle, but they don't know their destination.

I wrote this book to help fill that void.

Once you get to corporate America, you learn that if you don't have a vision for yourself and a plan for how to get there, you feel blind. You have to fit into a new culture fresh out of college, prove your worth, and advance in your career. It can be overwhelming, and you can feel out of place — like an imposter— if you don't have help. I didn't have help when I first entered the work force. But through my struggles and from advice from others, I learned how to find success in my career.

In this book, I've incorporated the experiences and knowledge I gained throughout my ten years in corporate America. You will learn skills, tools, and techniques that will help you stand out in your career and in your role. These are the basic fundamentals that will help you reach your goals.

This book can benefit millennials fresh out of college just entering the work force, seasoned vets who aren't where they want to be yet, and even people who are thinking about switching jobs of finding that career that really fits them.

Since we spend as much of our time at work as we do at home, and sometimes even more, it is important to find success in your career. So let me help you crush your work life. When you feel like you are really crushing it in one area of your life, you can find a greater sense of happiness.

You don't have to bump your head at every turn in your journey, like I did; instead, let me help you create a work GPS system to help you arrive safely at your destination and find that career satisfaction that you deserve.

# CHAPTER 1

---

# FINDING YOUR WHY — WHAT MOTIVATES YOU TO DO WHAT YOU DO?

Do you feel successful in your career? Fulfilled?

When I ask people this question, the answer is typically "no." It's a feeling that's rampant among professionals in the United States, especially among those considered part of the millennial generation. The jury is still out on *exactly* who comprises the millennial generation, but generally speaking, millennials were born from the early

1980's to around 2000. Which means, *yes*, I'm talking to YOU!

My next question is always: why do you do what you do? What drives you to work everyday?

The responses are often superficial:

1. I need to pay my bills.
2. I feel obligated because I need to support my family.
3. I don't want to let my parents down.
4. This is the job I fell into.
5. I don't think I can do better.

What you need to do is shift the why from the exterior to the interior. Why you do what you do shouldn't stem from an obligation, or pressure from a family member, or happenstance. In order for you to feel fulfilled by the work you do, the why of what you do needs to come from within you.

If work were taken out of it, if your parents weren't asking how work was going, if you didn't have bills to pay, and if you didn't have any obligations — what would you do? What inspires you on the most basic level? In other words, if there were something you could provide to the world through something you could do every day, what would that be?

What really drives you? What makes you motivated? What keeps you engaged?

I ask these questions because the thing that makes you tick **is embedded in who you are**. And the sooner you know who you are at your core, the sooner you can make a decision aligning your career with your inner self.

Through finding a career that's a good match for your inner self, you ultimately find fulfillment. And fulfillment is what gives you a feeling of success. So, let's work on finding your why so that you can get on a path that will ultimately give you fulfillment and success.

## Why?

There's this saying that I've heard many times before:

> "A life without purpose is a life not
> worth living."

I like to flip that:

> "A *career* without purpose, is a career
> not worth doing."

You have to be realistic about the meaning of having a career. A career is not just a thing you do to get money. That's a job. And if you're just going to get a job, you might as well get the easiest one possible that gets you money. But guess what? Even if it feels like it's what you want at first, ultimately, you don't just want a gig that will bring you money. Instead, you want to feel like you're adding value to the world with what you do. You want to feel like we have a purpose. You want to have a *career*.

Here's something that's really important to understand: money, when it's coming from a job that isn't making you feel like you have purpose, can only take you so far.

If you are reading this, there is a good chance that at some point in time, you have felt (or, if you haven't yet, there's a chance that you *will feel*) sure the money at your job would get you through. You were earning enough to pay your rent, to pay your student loans, and to have some fun on the side. But then you started dreading work. You started waking up in the morning wishing you didn't have to go to work. You started daydreaming about a job that would make you *feel better*.

Guess what? **That's how you know.** That's how you know that — money or not — the job you have isn't matching your why, and it isn't bringing you fulfillment. And the bottom line of that is simple: you aren't doing what you should be doing.

That's when it becomes necessary to get in touch with your why and find a career that's going to line up with it. Once your work is in line with your why, you're going to get up every morning excited to go make the difference that only you can make because of your unique point of motivation and inspiration.

Since America's higher education system doesn't discuss why you do what you do and how you, therefore, can find fulfillment, you may have come out of college with a degree that you can use, but discover you feel unfulfilled. Thus, you find yourself trapped and unsure of what to do. And because of this, a good number of millennials don't even put the degrees they earned to use. Did you know that studies have shown that a whopping 27% of people don't work in a field that's even related to their area of study?

# 'Why' As a Motivator

My sophomore year in college, I spent a lot of time fixated on making sure that I had a career when I graduated. I wanted to make sure I hit the ground running. However, I wasn't focused on my fulfillment. I was focused on making sure I had a job that was going to make me money the second I got out of school.

With this focus, I noticed that the people who interned at a lot of companies during college were the most successful at landing careers soon after graduating. Therefore, I made sure I interned at two, aligning myself for what I considered success. And I felt really comfortable going to graduation because both of the companies where I interned had sent me offers.

During the week of graduation, I received a call from the company whose offer I planned on accepting. They were calling to retract the offer they had made me due to the economy (this was in early 2007). I was shocked, and I was pissed, and I was scared. I immediately emailed the other company that had sent me an offer and told them that I was very interested in their offer. To my horror, they too told me they had to retract due to changes — mainly circumstances due to the economy.

Looking back at those two moments, I wish I'd had someone around to help guide me and my thoughts. If I could sit that version of myself down today, I'd say, "Dude, relax. Let's not just make moves for the hell of it. Let's regroup and come up with the next step forward."

However, I didn't have the current me to talk to, so instead of carefully deciding what to do next, I panicked. I didn't know what to do. And so I thought, "Whatever I got offered next, I would take." Not because whatever would come up next would be a good fit for me or because it would bring me fulfillment. No. I was just looking for something to grab hold to. I figured I'd figure the rest out later.

So, two weeks later, I ended up at a career fair. The owner of the venue came up to me and said, "Hey man, you really interview well. Are you still looking for a job?" I told him I hadn't decided on anything yet, and, right there, at that moment, he offered me a job. A couple of days passed by, and sure enough, he held true to his words. I got an offer letter that came in via email, and it was for $18,000. It was less than I should have been earning as a college graduate, but hey, like I said — I was in a panicked state, and I was ready to accept any offer that came my way. So I took it.

Because I had panicked, I accepted a job as a manager of the janitorial staff. I managed the crews that help open and close events. Shortly after starting, I was managing a John Deere Show, and it was clear that I'd had enough. It must have been on my face because my director brought me to his office and asked me if I liked the job. And staring at the puzzled look on my face, he said to me:

"You know what, you need to know the reason for doing what you're doing. You need to know why you do what you do."

It was the first time I'd ever heard anybody talk to me about having a why, having a reason, and that stuck with me. I knew in that instant that whatever my why was, I wasn't finding it at that job.

A couple of days later one of the corporations, a Fortune 500 company named Cerner, that I interviewed for during the career fair called me. I began working for them, and my why became money. I ended up getting a job as a test designer making $46,000 a year. I thought my why was solidified. I thought because I made $46,000 a year, I would be happy.

But even though this was a good job and it pay well, I had no interaction with people, and instead spent a lot of time in a cube, and I started to get depressed.

Money can only take you so far. At that point, my why was about the money. And, because it was about the money, I became depressed because money isn't everything. After a while, I don't care who you are, once you start making a little bit of money, and that's the only reason that you're getting up to go do what you do, you won't be doing it for long. You'll find somewhere else to go or you'll find yourself in bed wanting to not get up anymore.

And that's where I found myself. I found myself in bed often dragging myself out to go to work, dragging myself to get up because I no longer had a clear why. The lure of money had gone away.

One day my manager approached me, requesting I go on a special trip to visit a client. I would work directly with the client, show them how to use the software we had created, and, essentially, I'd get to see my hard work out on its feet.

That trip invigorated me in a huge way. It made me feel alive. What I didn't realize at the time is that on that trip, I was shaking hands with my 'why'.

My why is I love to help people: whether it's helping people understand how to use software to improve their business, consulting them, speaking at a big event, or coaching one on one, I love to help people.

When I discovered my why, I discovered what made me tick. I discovered what drove me, and it changed the course of my career. I was no longer all about the money. I had a sense of purpose and that drove me to excel.

Now, whether I'm speaking, consulting, coaching, or indulging my why in some other way, I get up every morning excited because I want to help folks. And I find ways to do that in everything I do. I don't take something on unless it's going to feed that passion.

When you know your why, you know what makes you tick. It gives you a sense of purpose. It gives you that energy that you need in the morning to get up because it drives you.

## How 'Why' affects Millennials in Corporate America

According to the 2015 U.S. Census, there are 83.1 million caffeinated and ready to change the world millennials roaming the US. That's a quarter of the nation's population. Ambitious, innovative, rule-breaking and risk-taking twenty and thirty somethings are ready to make their mark, and they want to do it in the millennial style.

Millennials seem to share an interesting set of characteristics:

1. They're not willing to settle for less.
2. They won't work for companies they don't respect.
3. They reinvent ways to climb the ladder.
4. They truthfully feel that money is not as important as being happy and balancing a healthy work and family life.
5. They tend to measure work by the output - not by the hours.

Despite these truths, the Bureau of Labor Statistics found that millennials between the ages of 18 and 28 have held an average of 7.2 jobs. Why?

We could easily point a finger and blame this trend on corporations who have missed the progressive wagon, welcoming the ME generation (Baby Boomers) through the doors of inflexible, developmentally stagnant, and socially irresponsible workplaces (which is absolutely partially the problem). But we would be remiss to not also acknowledge that part of the problem is that a lot of those in this energized age group of go-getters are "going to get" **without knowing why they're doing it.**

So this leads us to the big question: how do you make sure you don't fit the statistic and bounce around from job to job? How do you find the career that fits you and is going to give you long term fulfillment?

You know what I'm going to say: we need to find our why.

## How to Find Your Why

Now that I've told you why you need to get in touch with your why, let's get down to it. Go to a quiet place, free of distractions, where you can really think, and take out a piece of paper. For each of the questions below, really let yourself dream. Don't worry about how you sound - just brainstorm on the page. Let yourself discover your true feelings and thoughts about each of the questions below, and you'll be on your way to discovering your why.

1.  **What are your biggest strengths?**
    Don't just answer this like you're on a job interview — you don't need to impress anyone here. Really think about this. What are you good at? Are you a good listener? A

great cook? Are you good at lending perspective to others when they're going through some tough times? Forget all about money. Take money out of the equation. Just think about what you do in your day to day life that you're really good at and that you *enjoy*. What situation could you face and totally feel like, "Man. I've got this"?

2. **What are your unique skills?**
   What skills do you have? Are you a great typist? Great with communication? A musician? A computer whiz? Everyone has certain things they're good at, both emotionally and technically. What do you know a lot about and feel comfortable with?

3. **What makes you feel good? What do you enjoy?**
   Think about a moment when you feel like you've accomplished something. Like you're on a high. Something that no matter how many times you've done it, you still feel like doing it. Teaching someone something? Designing a website? Cooking a meal for your family? Working with technology? Working with people?

4. **What is at the core of your values?**
   How do you want to be viewed by others? Honest? Funny? Smart? Compassionate? Are you drawn to nature? To doing right by folks? To helping others? Knowing what's at the core of your being is going to help you find a company that shares those same values, which will help to feed your why.

After you've taken the time to answer the questions above, I want you to sit down and write a statement. When you know your why, it should be short. So sit down and come up with that short phrase that states your why. For example, my why statement proclaims, "I believe in helping passionate, driven individuals who want to excel in their lives and careers but aren't so sure on how to do so." And once you have that phrase, put it everywhere. Write it down and post it on your mirror. Make it the screensaver on your phone so you see it every time you pick the phone up. Remind yourself of your why daily so you will have this knowledge engrained completely.

The thing that you do for a living should give you some — if not all — of the joy you outlined above. If you said you want to be viewed as compassionate, then whatever you do for a living should allow you to be a compassionate person. The work you do should put your skills and strengths to work, and it should help you feel good about accomplishing whatever makes you feel best.

What's your why?

# Finding and Writing Your Why Statement

## STEP 1: BRAINSTORM

*Remember this is a brainstorming exercise, so do not judge your answers, just write everything down that comes to your mind.*

1.  What are your biggest strengths?

_____

_____

_____

2.  What are your unique skills?

_____

_____

_____

3. What makes you feel good? What do you enjoy?

_____

_____

_____

4. What is at the core of your values?

_____

_____

_____

## STEP 2: FIND YOUR WHY

*Go through your answers and look for a common theme. What idea/trait/concept appears in all four questions?*

Common ideas/themes:

_____

_____

_____

*Look over your common ideas/themes, and select the one that resonates the most with you to become your why. (My example: helping others)*

My why:

_____

_____

_____

## STEP 3: WRITE A WHY STATEMENT

*Once you have identified your why, you need to turn it into a sentence: write a clear, concise, bold why statement. (My example: I believe in helping passionate, driven individuals who want to excel in their lives and careers but aren't so sure on how to do so.)*

Why Statement:

_____

_____

_____

# CHAPTER 2

———— ∼ ————

# YOUR CAREER VISION: A PATH TO YOUR FUTURE

O nce you know your why, it's time to build a career vision.

Many go into their careers with no end in sight, and some go into our careers with visionless lofty goals. I speak from personal experience. At one point about two years into a consulting career, I attended a workshop with my company. During the networking portion, everyone had a few drinks and then sat around and talked to each other. The subject got around to where everyone saw themselves a few years down the road in their careers. And that's when I said, without hesitation and very matter-of-factly, "I'm going to be a senior consultant."

That's when John, my supervisor, gave me a look. But I didn't see the look because I was too busy blabbing away about all that I had done up to that point and how all of that meant that I should be a senior consultant. Of course, none of what I was talking about meant that I should make the leap from where I was at that moment to senior consultant - it just meant I had done what I needed to do to get myself to my current point. I was being cocky and bold — two stereotypes of millennials.

John, who was wiser than me, didn't confront me right there. Later, though, he pulled me aside and privately said, "I think you're a great person. Where are you at in the process of becoming a senior consultant?"

That gave me pause. I said, "I'm sorry?" I didn't get it.

He asked again, "Where are you at in the process? What have you done that would qualify you for senior consultant?"

I blinked at him and said, "I don't know."

His answer? "If you don't know where you are at in the process to becoming a senior consultant, it's less than likely that you'll get there."

In the moment, that stung. But later when I thought about it, I got what he meant. In truth, I hadn't shadowed a senior consultant — I didn't actually know what they did, other than they seemingly did something more important than my job. I saw what other people were doing in that position, and I just blindly said, "I could do that!" I hadn't researched the qualifications of the job. That's another thing millennials tend to do —see someone else doing something and just assume they could do that too.

As with just about any journey in life, if you don't know how you're going to get there, it is less than likely that you're going to get there.

So, this encounter switched up my frame of mind. I decided to start taking all of my visions and started to attack them backwards instead of forward. So, the evening after I had that conversation with the director, I went home. I took a piece of paper, and I wrote, "Senior consultant, how do I obtain this measure? How do I get to this point?"

I started writing down all the skill sets I felt like I needed to have, the things I needed to achieve, the certification I needed to obtain; things I needed to know, knowledge I needed to have to make myself senior consultant material.

I figured out that the first thing I had to do was get myself prepared in all aspects to demand that type of position. And then after that, I started figuring out what steps I needed to take in the process to get to that point, working it backwards.

It's a big deal to be able to work your vision backwards. And in doing so, not only did I obtain my goal of becoming a senior consultant, but this thinking led me to opening up my own consulting business.

I've seen a lot of young professionals who are exactly like I was in my early career. I spent a lot of time doing the same thing, the same exact thing over and over and over again because I hadn't mapped out a road to success. Without a plan, you will end up repeating yourself for multiple years whereas if you had a plan, you could be moving forward in much less time. After several years in my consulting career, I created a plan, and I made my goal in a year and a half. A year and a half! That's pretty incredible. And I did it by first working my vision backwards so that I knew each and every step I needed to take.

## Why Vision Matters

Vision matters because it keeps you out of the dark.

When you have a vision for your life and career, you're able to think five, ten, fifteen steps ahead. When you have no vision whatsoever, you can't see what the next move is. It's a lot like playing chess. People that are great chess players think several moves ahead — they know what possibilities and obstacles lie ahead of them on their way to a checkmate. If you are going to obtain the goals you want in your career, you have to have a vision because it allows you to move a few steps ahead.

If you don't have that, you're walking in the wilderness just hoping that you get lucky enough to bump into your goal.

In most careers, we begin in a lower position than the position we ultimately would like to have. More times than not, our starting position isn't something we necessarily like or want to do forever. This makes sense — it motivates us to strive to achieve within the career so that we can be promoted and move up the ranks. The thing is, though, if you don't have a vision for wanting to move up, or expand to a different role, then you are going to sit stagnant in that role. If there isn't something that role would get you — i.e. a promotion you want to obtain — you aren't going to strive to do your best in that role.

In order to be fulfilled at each stage of your career, from the entry level position all the way on up, you need to have a sense of where you want to end up. Knowing what promotions to strive for, and what paths you need to take to get those promotions, helps you move up in the ranks on the path to your ultimate goal. Knowing what you need to do (and what to avoid doing) helps you do your best in each position you're in so that you can get the recognition you need to move beyond it. It helps you remember that y**our right now isn't your later.**

Visioning is something humans possess that makes us unique. We are able to imagine a future that we wish we had, and we are able to work toward it. As a professional, it's important that you take advantage of this human talent and craft a vision for your future. You need to let that vision be a motivator for you throughout every stage of your career so that you can gain fulfillment and knowledge each step of the way, ultimately making you a better professional in the now and in the future.

The people that I've seen excel in their careers and in their lives were those who had a vision.

If I were to tell you to make a paper airplane and throw it at the target, would you be able to hit it? No, you would stand there confused, wondering what target you should hit. But if I were to tell you to throw it at a certain picture, could you do that? Yes, you might not hit it directly depending on how good your aim is, but since you have a clear target, you would come close. That is what a vision does for you. It gives you a clear target.

If you don't choose a vision for yourself, your company will chose your position for you. You have to know what position you want and reach to obtain it.

Vision matters because it gives you control of your destiny.

## Planning Your Legacy

In surveys, many millennials state that leaving a lasting impact on the world is most important to them.

Knowing what you'd like to be known for can be really helpful in determining the vision you want for your career. One way to think about this is — what would you like your career obituary to say? In the end, how do you want the work you did to be summed up?

For me, I've always wanted to be known for helping others. I like the feeling I get when I've helped somebody figure something out. I love creating impact for people — helping people find those "ah ha" moments — for their lives and careers. I like helping people find their place in the world. I like helping people figure out who they are at their core.

What is it for you? Do you want to add to the field you work in and leave it better than you found it? Do you want to leave a remembrance of what you did for your company or for other people? Did you leave behind a remembrance of what you did for your company or for other people?

## How To Get There

If you were handed a map right now and your career destination was marked with an X, could you pinpoint where you currently are on the journey? Are you a quarter of the way there? Half way? Have you wandered off the trail into the woods?

When I'm coaching millennials, most **cannot tell me where they are on their map** because they have not worked their vision backwards. They have not figured out the steps it will take to get to where they want to go. They just know where they want to end up, and they're trying to do what they think is right, hoping it'll magically land them where they want to go.

To get to where you want to go, you have to be a lot more specific than just doing what you think is right and hoping for the best. Without knowing the steps you need to take, you can't take action on achieving those steps, which means you're bound to take a lot longer than you need to in order to get to your end game.

Let's take a simple example. In middle school, I was asked to write the steps for a peanut butter and jelly sandwich, and I failed to get all the steps in. Let's trace the steps backwards.

Okay, so how do you do that? You have to go through a series of steps. The easiest way to map out those steps is to go backwards.

End: Eat the sandwich.

What comes before that? Let's envision this. Right before I eat that sandwich, I put the two pieces of bread together. Right before that, I spread peanut butter on one side. Before that, I put a knife in the peanut butter jar to bring the peanut butter to the bread. Before that, I unscrewed the top of the peanut butter to be able to get the knife in there. Before that, I grabbed the peanut butter jar, the bread, and a knife from wherever they were all kept in my kitchen. Before that, I did all the same things with the jelly. That's a lot of steps. And although making a PB&J sandwich might be something you don't think about in steps as you're doing it, when you're forced to think about the steps, you start to realize without the progression of each step, you would never get to the end product.

Back when I did this exercise in middle school, I forgot tons of important steps. I forgot to unscrew the top of the jelly. I forgot to take the knife out. I forgot to unscrew the peanut butter top. I was so focused on that sandwich that I was unable to envision the steps it would take me to get there.

One of the biggest problems people face when planning is completely underestimating the amount of time it will take to accomplish their goal. In a study conducted on directional planning, researchers found that planning backwards increased attention to circumstantial delays like obstacles, competing demands, and interruptions whereas those who planned in a traditional start to end manner ended up with what researchers call the optimistic bias. While optimism is good, being realistic with your expectations, timeline, and possible interferences is even better.

So, what does it take to create a vision that actually works? You don't have to just take a shot in the dark and hope that you "get lucky" to be successful. Luck, after all, is where preparation meets opportunity.

## Taking Steps

Let's get practical. Below are the steps you need to take in order to map out your career vision and how you're going to get there.

After each step in the process ask yourself, how did I get here? Untangle each question carefully and thoroughly.

**Step 1: Identify your career vision.**

Picture your life three years from now. You want to only look three years ahead rather than ten or fifteen because you want to tackle your life and career in small, attainable chunks. Maybe you want to be a CEO in fifteen years, but hey - let's take that one step at a time. Fifteen years is a long time to map out. Instead, let's look three years ahead toward someone who is maybe also on track to becoming a CEO.

Okay, so — three years from now: picture it. What do you see? Revel in the details. Who are you working for? What are you doing? Where are you? Are you happy? What kind of new skills and training have you taken on? What is your "big picture"? Pretend like you already lived it, and you're recalling a memory. This vision should make you feel energized and peaceful and give you a sense of "I made it."

**Step 2: Create strategies to lay the foundation.**

Some goals are critical to your success. If you want to be a doctor and you don't go to medical school - well, that's a problem. This would be considered a strategic move, one that you can't meet your career goal without it.. If you don't go to medical school, you have zero percent chance of becoming one.

Work backwards from your vision in step 1 and identify the milestones you know you absolutely have to do to get to the X on your map.

**Step 3: Break down your strategies into a series of smaller goals for each one working backwards from the end-game.** Intermediary goals are just as important as the greater vision itself. Clearly, without medical school you cannot become a doctor, but what about the steps you have to take to get into medical school? Stepping stones are crucial to keep your focus clear and less overwhelming. Imagine checking off a step like "apply to medical school" instead of "become a doctor" - it just seems more reasonable and more manageable. Plus, you can actually use these intermediary goals as a metric to measure your success (and identify your waypoint on your vision map).

**Step 4: Break down the intermediary goals into identifiable action plans.**

Each goal needs a relative action/plan to get checked off. What do you actually have to do to knock out the goal which in turn will lead to the critical milestone? To apply for medical school (the goal) you probably need to gather references (action plan) and write an essay (action plan).

**Step 5: Write down foreseeable obstacles, proposed solutions, and needed resources.**

Write down things that might keep you from achieving your milestones. For example, if you cannot currently afford a class or tuition needed to complete your degree or obtain the needed certification, you should identify money as an obstacle and plan out steps you can take to earn the money or obtain a school loan.

Some obstacles, like needing money for your certification and/or degree, are easy to identify. There may be some obstacles, though, that you don't know about yet, but you could still plan for. This is where your mentor can help. Ask him or her the obstacles he or she faced on the same journey so you can identify more obstacles.

If you can't find someone in person who you can talk to, check out books written by people in the field you want to enter. You may be able to get a sense of the foreseeable journey that way, too.

**Step 6: Take action and define the timeline.**

Having the blueprints to a building only means something if you start to build. Define the timeline. This should be a realistic yet committed approach to reaching your goals. Life happens, so if you fall off track a bit - it's okay, you're human. Do your best to stick to the plan, reassessing where you are at least twice a year until your vision is no longer a distant illusion, but the present.

Sequence the steps out. You can do this by numbering them, color coding them, or writing on sticky notes and moving them around (kind of like a detective creates a storyboard for a crime). This is an involved process that will force you to put more thought and meaning behind your planning - and it can be a lot of fun.

## Flexible Vision

Your career vision is a living document. It's kind of like the Constitution — it will change over time. You're going to need to add amendments to accommodate your growing vision. This vision will be fluid. It may change three years from now as you meet new people, learn new information, and formulate new plans - and that's okay. In fact, it's encouraged. You may meet the love of your life, get married and then realize that his or her passions matched with your passions could create a whole new and improved vision you never imagined before. Let it happen. Just remember to assess your path often, like checking for a trail marker, to make sure you're still heading in the right direction.

Ask yourself a few questions as you sit down to put your vision to paper:

- What do you want your life to look like in 3 years? (review this and create a new vision every 3 years)
- What habits would you need to adopt to make this vision of your future self a reality? Which habits would you need to kick?
- Are you currently in a position that is contributing to your future success? If not, what can you do to get out of the woods and back on track?
- Why is reaching this goal important to you? Find your why and use it as a tool to motivate you towards your vision.
- What kind of support will you need to make it through, emotionally, financially and intellectually?
- Thinking back on your life as if you made it - what are some important decisions you would have made along the way that brought you to where you are?
- What will be your legacy? If you were reading your obituary in the paper, what would you want it to say about your career accomplishments?

Consider creating a career vision board, a collection of everything that inspires you, energizes you, and that reminds you of what you're fighting for. People without a cohesive vision can become trapped in the day-to-day monotony of life forgetting to put one foot in front of the other. They may have once had a big picture vision, but it got lost as they struggled to keep afloat. Remember, a vision unraveled backwards can be your saving grace.

Don't limit yourself to what has been done before - be creative, think outside of the box, and know that all of the most successful people have taken educated risks.

## Creating Your Strategies, Goals, and Plans

Here I have shown you the steps necessary to map out your vision. Since each of those steps are crucial, in the next chapter I have laid out more instructions on how to create these strategies, goals, and plans.

Begin at the end, take a SMART (specific, measurable, achievable, realistic and time-bound) approach to being successful in your professional life and remember that tomorrow is going to come anyway, it's a matter of what you do with it that counts.

# CHAPTER 3

───────── ∼ ─────────

# YOUR CAREER GPS: GOALS, PLANS, AND STRATEGIES

So, I've talked about discovering your "why," and I've talked about building your career vision, laying out the steps to help you get there. I've talked with so many people who entered corporate America without any real goals or strategies. They just knew they were earning a paycheck, and in their minds, they figured they were doing "the right thing." With no real direction, though, most of these people found themselves at one point or another totally dissatisfied and overwhelmed.

It's kind of like if you were to say, "I know vacationing is important for recharging and relaxing, which sounds fulfilling, so I'm going to go on a vacation." Okay, but where are you going to go? You wouldn't just hop in the car and drive and call that a vacation. Instead, you pick out a place, you plug the address into our GPS, and you follow the directions of the journey until you get to where you've decided to go.

**Your career is the same way.** You can't just say "I'm going to have a fruitful and exciting career" and expect to hop in your career car and go. You have to have a destination, and you have to follow the correct steps to reach that destination. In the last chapter, I outlined all the steps. Within those steps are critical elements that will help you get anywhere you need to go.

I call those critical elements the **career GPS:**

**G**oals
**P**lans
**St**rategies

There's a good chance that without a map to tell you how to get to where you want to go, you've experienced some of the feelings that many millennials have:

- *What am I doing?*
- *Where am I really trying to go?*
- *Am I on the right path or am I just wasting time?*
- *Why can't I seem to get it together?*

If you've had these thoughts, trust me — you are not alone.

We all want to be successful in one way or another. It's how you choose to tackle the journey that makes the difference between whether or not your goals are realized. So what can you do to try and move career mountains? Strategize. Plan. Execute.

## Being Intentional

It's easy to let a bunch of ideas swirl around in your mind, but until you set a true intention to define those ideas as goals, they aren't solid, and you aren't working toward them. I've found in my own practice that writing down my goals is the best way to solidify them and make them real and tangible.

The mere act of writing can almost create a muscle memory to remind you of its creation. Also, this puts it in black and white, which as an actionable step in and of itself, makes your goal a real, living, breathing thing.

A few years back, I had it in my mind that I wanted to increase my revenue to over $100,000. That was just an idea when it was in my head, but then I wrote that goal down. Suddenly, this concept became something real that I was working toward. (Similarly, you might think about getting a new job, but once you're actually writing a cover letter to apply, the idea now becomes a goal that you're acting on.) With that goal set, I was able to then create strategies and put plans into place to see that goal from idea to reality.

A study on goal-setting done by a Dominican University professor, Dr. Gail Matthews, provided empirical evidence that physically writing down goals, strategies, and plans increases success rates by almost 25%. If you manage to rope in a supportive friend who will listen to your goal progress once a week - you're 65% more likely to be successful reaching your goal than those who don't share and don't write it down. Over the years I've had many accountability partners for various goals. People I have shared my goals with and who have held me liable by checking in with me periodically to check my progress. Having someone who had an interest in my goal achievement and who made sure that I was staying on my toes made a huge impact for me. If you can find someone who is willing to hold you accountable, you will be that much better off in your quest for your goal.

## Developing a Strategy

Remember the first time you decided to move out on your own? When you left the comforts of home-cooked meals and the security of free shelter? I bet that at least someone in your life doubted whether or not you could make it out on your own — a parent, a grandparent, a neighbor -- someone. If you were anything like me, you were hell-bent on making it. And so in that moment, you wanted to make it out on your own, whatever it took. Your strategy for success became simple: survive.

To do this, you probably spun a bunch of plans without realizing it:

- You found your own place
- You got a job to pay your rent
- You bought food *and* you learned how to cook that food

Your strategy to survive pushed you to make plans and to put those plans into action.

Now let's apply this same principle to defining your path to career success. Let's say your vision is to become a director within a big corporation. But right now, you're in an entry level position within the corporation. It's paying the bills, but it's definitely not what you want to be doing for the rest of your life.

So what's your strategy? It could be:

- Find out what is required of directors. What skills do you need to have in order to get that job?
- Learn anything and everything you can about the position.
- Find out everything you can about your company's approach to advancement within the company. This will help you discover in advance things that may have otherwise been unforeseen obstacles.
- Learn from others who have climbed the ladder. Look at their mistakes and experiences.
- Network with colleagues and peers. Talk to people who have gone from where you are now to where you're trying to go.

The object of developing a strategy is to lay out the conditions that will favor success.

Now ask yourself: what will you have to do to reach your unique professional goals? What will it take?

Write down a career strategy to jump-start your own liberation. Hang on to this because it will become the container that holds the array of plans needed to execute your goal.

Strategy is not a consequence of planning, but the opposite - it's the starting point.

## Developing Goals

A year and a half into my career in corporate America, I had become depressed. I felt like I was doing the same thing over and over and that I wasn't living up to my potential. I ended up going on a company trip that put me in direct contact with clients. The trip made me feel really inspired and energized, and out of that, I realized that long term I wanted to become a consultant, which would allow me to work directly with clients all the time.

Becoming a consultant became the vision that informed the moves I made. So I had to create a strategy to make that happen. My strategy was to shadow a consultant. Then within that strategy, I had to break it down into clear goals.

Goals help you get to where you are going. While your strategy is your big idea, you have to ensure you know the how. In order to make it happen, you need to set clear SMART goals.

**Specific:** What exactly is your goal? Answer the who, what, and where. This step usually involves verbs like "develop" or "create."

**Measurable:** How will you measure your steps to success? Create objectives for each goal to be milestones along your path. What will these milestones look like?

**Achievable**: Challenge yourself to step outside of your comfort zone. What is a reasonable goal for you?

**Relevant:** How does this goal relate to your larger career goals or life goals? Is this a worthwhile goal to strive for? How will it change you or meet your needs?

**Time-bound:** What does the timeline for your goal look like? A week? Two weeks? A month? A year? Time-management skills are crucial in the goal-setting process.

## Developing Plans

You've probably planned a thing or two in your life. You may plan to meet friends for drinks after work, or plan to deliver a presentation at a conference, or plan to call clients for feedback. The keywords here being meet, deliver, and call. They are verbs that indicate some kind of action is taking place.

Plans are the actionable steps you take to reach a set goal: they are the how, the who, and the when.

Plans will fall nicely inside the confines of a well-designed goal. Imagine unpacking the goal into a to-do list.

If your vision is to move up the corporate ladder, then your goal could be to become a valuable asset to the company, and within that goal, your plans could include:

- Create impact in your current position — excel in what you're doing right now. You want your organization to recognize your value.
- Contact people who are in the positions you want to be in and seek mentorship from them.
- Make impactful connections with coworkers,

clients, and others. You want your coworkers and your superiors to recognize your abilities as a leader and as a member of the same team who has intentions to be a part of the family, so to speak, long term.

Plans are essentially tasks that add up to something bigger than themselves. Picture a ladder. The strategy is the frame of the ladder, and plans are the rungs that help you climb the ladder. Conquer one plan at a time as you hold onto the strategy for support. Sometimes the plans will change, and that's okay. Where there is a Plan A, there is always a Plan B - even if you don't know it yet.

Have that strategy you wrote down handy? Beneath your strategy, write down all of the steps it's going to take to get there, and then make a plan for each one. How will you achieve everything needed to get to the top of the ladder?

## Changing Plans

In creating my own SMART goals, I decided that the best plan I could enact would be to shadow someone who was already acting as a consultant at the company, so that I could learn and ask questions about the job. I also made sure that I continued to excel in my current position, and I got in touch with the person who had the power to advance me within the company, letting her know that I was interested in this type of promotion. I was ultimately told no — they didn't think that I would be good in that position.

I was crushed. My plan had not worked. But the strategy driving me remained the same — I still knew that I wanted to be a consultant, which meant that I needed to come up with a new plan as to how to get there. Sometimes even with a GPS guiding you, you're going to encounter roadblocks and detours, and you're going to need to navigate around them and come up with a new plan for how to get to where you're going.

I ended up taking some time away from that work, regrouping and reconfiguring my goals and plans. Eventually, I worked as a third party consultant, which allowed me to experience the role that I knew I wanted. In taking this path, one I hadn't initially expected to take, I achieved my goals in bigger and better ways than I had ever initially envisioned. So although my first plan didn't necessarily get me to where I wanted to go, by keeping that strategy at the forefront of my efforts, I still remained true to myself and landed where I had wanted all along.

You are likely going to grow and change along the course of your journey, and your goals, plans, and strategies are going to grow with you. When things feel uncertain or overwhelming, keep your map — and the fact that you can create one anytime you need one — at the forefront of your mind. You are the leader of the journey you are on, and you have the ability to dictate that journey, whatever it may be.

So have at it. Design your success story. Take educated risks, strive to make change, and stay committed to the ride.

## Mapping Out Your Career Vision & Your GPS

STEP 1: MAP OUT YOUR VISION AND YOUR GPS TO GET THERE

*Go through steps 1-5 laid out in Chapter 2 and map out your career vision. Identify your vision, the critical milestone(s), the intermediary goal(s), the plan(s) with clear actions you need to take, and the foreseeable obstacles with solutions and resources.*

*Example: (on a small scale example, let's imagine you want to shadow a potential mentor, so you can assess your needed long-term goals and plan your journey. This is a basic example, but the principle remains the same as you scale it up to larger issues like getting into your favored university or getting a promotion. )*

**Vision:** *to shadow a mentor for a few days to get a sense of his or her job and to ask questions about his or her journey*

**Strategy #1:** *find a mentor to shadow*

> **Intermediary SMART goal:** *get permission from mentor to shadow and schedule the dates it's going to happen*

> **Plans towards goal:** *call or email the mentor - make a connection, introduce yourself, and ask if shadowing might be a possibility*

> **Foreseeable Obstacles:** *time conflicts, not the right mentor, mentor doesn't meet all needs*

>> *Solutions: Ask the potential mentor questions before hand to assess whether he or she is the right mentor, craft a clear email outlining my needs, objectives, and goals for the mentorship, find out mentor's availability and reschedule other events to allow for mentorship meetings*

>> *Resources: email, personal connections,*

*chapter 7 of this book*

**You may have more strategies and intermediary goals than the worksheet allows for, so it is best to complete this on your own paper, below is a sample outline you can complete on your own paper.**

Vision:

Strategy #1:

    Intermediary goal#1:

        Plan(s) towards goal:

        Foreseeable Obstacles:

            Solutions:

            Resources:

    Intermediary Goal #2:

        Plan(s) towards goal:

        Foreseeable Obstacles:

            Solutions:

            Resources:

Strategy #2:

Intermediary goal#1:

Plan(s) towards goal:

Foreseeable Obstacles:

Solutions:

Resources:

Intermediary Goal #2:

Action(s) towards goal:

Foreseeable Obstacles:

Solutions:

Resources:

ETC.....

## STEP 2: DEFINE THE TIMELINE

*Go back and write a due date for each of your action steps, goals, and milestones. This will just be a rough guide, roughly when do you need to tackle each piece in order to meet your vision in three years.*

# CHAPTER 4

———————⟨~⟩———————

# TIME MANAGEMENT

I grew up with a really weak sense of time management. My parents had very little sense of time. If there was a family party starting at four, we would show up around five, without stressing over our tardiness. My parents just didn't think that being on time was necessary. Growing up witnessing a lazy attitude towards punctuality, I kind of absorbed my parents' attitudes and didn't care about time efficiency.

Until I joined the military.

In the military, your day is planned down to the minute, and if you are someone who isn't great with time, you learn how to be — and fast. Gone were the days of not minding my time.

When I returned back to the workforce after being in the military, I felt myself slipping back into my old ways and wasn't efficient with my time. One day, one of my mentors asked me how I ever survived the military lacking time management skills. I said that I had done what I had to do there, and she asked why I couldn't take the principles I had learned in the military and apply them to my work.

From that day forward, I have made a careful effort to employ some basic techniques for keeping myself on point with my work and schedule. Learning how to manage your time efficiently is a cornerstone for success.

Here, I'll talk about the struggles I've had with various aspects of time management and what techniques I have used in order to mange and overcome those struggles.

## 1. Plan Your Day

I don't believe in planning your day when you wake up. I have found after much trial and error that I am much more efficient if at the end of each workday, I make a plan for what I am going to do the next day.

That way when I come into a new workday with a fresh mind, my to-do list is already waiting for me. I already have a plan, which means I don't have to get flustered creating one. I'm there, and I'm ready to dive in.

When I first started my career, I didn't know about the power of planning the day. I always felt like there wasn't enough time in the day, which gave me a ton of anxiety and frustration. In that time in my life, I met a football coach, Coach Mac, and he swore by planning your day out the night before. He taught me how to do it, and I have to say, it totally transformed how I do my work. It's a lot like a football game, actually. Rather than going out on the field and winging it, I'm going in with a plan for a series of plays that'll get me to the end zone.

Planning your day takes the mystery out of what you will do during your work day. If you're just sitting at your desk wondering what you should do next, it's nearly impossible to make the most of your time.

When I make my lists, I tend to break my day up into three to five things that I need to work on and accomplish. Now, that doesn't always mean finishing a task from start to finish. Sometimes, it might mean starting with something smaller. But it also might mean that I work it out so that I need to spend at least an hour toward finishing something larger. Chipping away at larger projects one bit at a time is just as much an accomplishment as starting and finishing a smaller task all at once.

It helps to work out your day in both time and tasks. Typically you know how much time you intend to spend working in a day. In addition to knowing what tasks you need to accomplish, it helps to plan out what chunks of that time will be dedicated to which tasks.

Mapping out your day might sound routine and robotic, but the most successful people *are* very routine. Routines are the pillars that give you the stability to succeed.

## 2. Prioritize

As it relates to your career, getting your priorities in order is really important, and it's often overlooked.

When it comes to priorities, you need to understand the difference between the Must Do's and the Want To's (and there is a big difference!). What do you **need** to do in order to succeed in your current position? What do you **need** to do in order to work toward advancing in your career while still succeeding in your current position? As we have discussed in other chapters, there are certain things that we delineate for ourselves as necessities for advancing in the ways that we want to advance. Those are your Must Do's.

We all have tons of Want To's, and let's be honest — a lot of times it feels easier and happier in the moment to focus on those Want To's. Going on social media, for example. Taking a longer lunch than usual with a friend. Even working on a non-essential work project can sometimes fall under the "Want To" category.

When it comes to priorities, the Must Do's need to be the priority. And until those priorities are handled, that Want To list shouldn't really even be touched.

Look — I've been there. I've been the guy that's sitting in the office while the rest of the team is out at a happy hour together. I've also been the guy who shirked his priorities while saying over and over that I wanted to advance; I wanted to get to a certain level; I wanted to give my work my all. But until I was actually giving it my all — prioritizing the Must Do's over the Want To's — I wasn't able to make the advances that I so badly wanted to accomplish.

## 3. Task Management

Scientifically, it's been proven that true multitasking — doing a ton of unrelated things at once — is virtually impossible. There's no way that anybody can fully focus on one thing while fully focusing on another thing. You might be able to dabble in two things at once, but in that instance, you can't really give a task or a goal your all. You need to focus on things one at a time.

I like to think about this in terms of the internet. Broadband or high speed internet is like hyper focus. You're getting things done and you're getting them done fast because you are only focusing on that one thing. Multitasking, on the other hand, is more like dial up or a modem. You're working through the information, but each thing is happening slower. Since you aren't giving one thing your all, you can't get it done with the efficiency or focus that you could if you were only doing that one thing.

However, I think there's a way to make multitasking work for you. When we think about the larger tasks that we accomplish in a day, we can also think about the smaller tasks under the umbrella of that bigger task. If you try to focus on simultaneous tasks that are working toward different ends, it's really hard to give it your all. Everything we focus on should be in the same task family. So, you can select a big task and work on five smaller things that you need to accomplish in order to check that larger task off your list.

I like to organize my day so that I'm doing a few mini tasks in the morning — things that won't take me a ton of time, but that ultimately contribute to what I want to accomplish overall during the day. Accomplishing smaller tasks gives me energy and confidence that I'm getting what I need to get done that day, and that I'm going to be able to finish my bigger tasks, too. These smaller tasks are not time consuming; are often related to the bigger task; and they sometimes, can happen simultaneously. Also, I try to make sure that all of those smaller tasks relate to the bigger task that I'm going to accomplish later, which helps streamline my thought process so that it's all focused on that one area of my work.

When I am focusing on a bigger task, I try to give it my complete focus. I don't have anything that I'm doing other than focusing on that big task at hand.

So, to give an example — I used to think that I was multitasking (and therefore was at ultimate productivity) by trying to accomplish a ton of different things at once. Usually, those things were not related to one another, which meant that my brain was not able to really focus on one aspect of work. It was trying to be everywhere at one time. In one day, I would work on a chapter of my book at home and then drive to other side of town to meet with my coach to rehearse and craft my speeches, and then I would have my podcast show review. As a result, I was all over the place. I wasn't getting anything done efficiently. I was getting to the end result a lot slower.

I find that in today's day and age, it's really hard to give yourself that type of hyper focus. It's so easy to pick up the phone and text or click onto social media while you're trying to work on one thing. However, it is so important that you turn all of that off — even just for a small increment of time — to give yourself that serious focus on one task. Laser focus is what's going to make you efficient.

## 4. Combat Procrastination

Procrastination is something that afflicts most millennials. And it's not just you — this is pretty much a common human condition. Tackling tasks as soon as you can instead of waiting until later may be a constant battle for you, and for many of us.

A few years ago, I decided to actively combat procrastination in my life. I didn't just say "I'm not going to procrastinate anymore" — I decided that I needed to employ techniques to really find ways to actively battle this force that crept up for me so often.

For me personally, working from home causes procrastination. If I'm home, there are too many distractions around me, and I have a ton of trouble actually focusing on the topics I need to focus on. So, for me, I had to remove myself from any situation where I would be working at home. If I put myself in a place where I am there solely to focus on the work — a cafe, a library, an office — then I have an easier time focusing on that task.

Your environment can have a huge impact on your productivity and your inspiration, so being in touch with how that affects you is a great first line of defense against procrastination. And this doesn't just apply to when and if youwork from home, either all the time or occasionally. Procrastination can also find you at the office. Maybe your desk is in a particularly loud part of the office, or maybe your desk is adjacent to a friend who you often find yourself talking to. It's important you address whatever might be standing in the way of your productivity. Many offices have alternate spaces that you can work in such as a conference room or another quiet area.

I've also found that in addition to paying attention to my environment, I need to pay attention to my dress. If I'm not dressed for success, I find it easier to goof off. The way that I am presenting myself and the way the world sees me affects my work on a subconscious level. So even if I am not meeting with clients for the day, I dress as though I am. When I feel like I'm at work, I have an easier time focusing on work.

My timeline and to-do list really helps me to not procrastinate, too. Anytime I feel myself slipping into that place of feeling bored or feeling like I need to fill my mind with some fluff, I look to that to-do list, which is really a guide that tells me what I need to be doing at any given moment.

Above all, don't let yourself off the hook. If you know that working in particular environments doesn't work for you, try your best to find alternate environments to work in. If you know you need to feel like you're playing the part, then do whatever you need to do and wear whatever you need to wear so that you feel the way you need to feel. If you know you have tasks on that to-do list, don't stop until they're done.

Don't forgive yourself if you don't. Hold yourself accountable.

## 5. Break it Up

I work breaks into my overall workday schedule, which helps me to recharge and stay focused. For example, if I'm breaking up my to-do list into one hour increments, I work for fifty minutes, and then I take a ten minute break.

Taking that break allows me to recharge and maybe indulge in some of the activities that I refrained from doing during my fifty minutes of true work time. In order to stay on point, you should break up your schedule and plan your day to allow you to stay within the blocks of time dedicated for each task.

When you're taking a break from work, make sure that you're physically engaging yourself. Get up and walk around. Stretch. Go to the window or step outside for some fresh air. Getting your body up and moving will give you a boost of energy that will really help you when you get back to your work.

Make sure that you have something that you can use at the end of your ten minute break to get you back in the zone, focused, and ready to go. Maybe it's a quote that really gets you energized about your work, or a mantra you say to yourself to get yourself pumped. Create a smooth transition to draw you back to your work, almost like a pre-game routine. Something that you do to get yourself in the zone.

# In Conclusion

Proper time management is a skill that you have to practice again and again and work really hard at. Eventually, with enough time and effort, these techniques will become habits — things you do because you're used to doing them. But make no mistake: at the beginning, time management may seem hard! It *is* hard. With enough effort and focus, though, you can integrate these techniques into your work life and ultimately come out more efficient and more successful for it.

Proper time management skills can be really liberating. When you no longer find yourself running around in your head trying to figure out what you should be doing and when, you will thank yourself for working hard at rewiring your brain to adapt to these skills and techniques.

# Plan Your Day

## STEP 1: IDENTIFYING TASKS

*Complete step 1 as often as needed. (Could be every month or every week depending on how you like to plan)*

1. What are your big projects?

_____     _____

_____     _____

2. Take each big project and break it up into smaller tasks.

Big Project #1: _____

Small Task: _____

Small Task: _____

Small Task: _____

Big Project #2: _____

Small Task: _____

Small Task: _____

Small Task: _____

3. What are some of your other tasks you need to accomplish this month or week (whatever chunk of time you are working with)?

_____

_____

_____

## STEP 2: PRIORITIZE YOUR TASKS

*Go through your list of tasks and determine which ones need to be done first and which ones can wait a while. Next to each task either write the due date or write the order it needs to be completed (writing a 1 next to the task you need to do first etc).*

## STEP 3: CREATE DAILY PLAN

*This step should be completed nightly, so you are ready the next day. List the tasks you will do tomorrow and roughly how long you will spend on each task.*

*Example:*

Work on Project 1 for an hour
Read and reply to emails for 30 mins
Take 10 min break

Work on Project 2 for an hour
Send out meeting invites for any meetings with team or manager for 30 mins
Take 10 min break
Prepare for meetings for 30 minutes
Go back and complete needed task for Project 1 or 2 for rest of day

_____

_____

_____

_____

_____

_____

_____

_____

_____

_____

_____

# CHAPTER 5

~

# SOFT SKILLS

Non-technical skills are referred to as *soft skills*. Technical skills that you need to obtain in order to find yourself in a specific career (for example, a degree) are referred to as hard skills. Hard skills are, of course, necessary and important. They're how you achieve the knowledge you need in order to perform necessary tasks within your career. However, soft skills are one of the most heavily overlooked factors when determining what makes one person succeed in a career over another. CEOs and human resource managers report millennials tend to lack these soft skills.

To put this into some perspective, let's talk about

how soft skills might play into our daily lives. Let's say that I'm picking a new doctor. I'll likely look at the doctors that my insurance covers, and I'll pick one to meet. Now, I'm probably going to go ahead and assume that the doctor has indeed completed medical school and has a medical degree. (Otherwise, he or she would not be able to practice medicine.) So, even though the hard skill of earning a degree likely dominated that doctor's life for many years while he or she was in school, I'm honestly almost going to take it for granted — at the very least, it isn't what's going to be the focus of my visit to the doctor.

When I visit that doctor for the first time and I'm vetting whether or not this is someone whom I want to make my primary care physician, I'm going to be looking at his or her bedside manner. Is the doctor a good communicator? Does he or she seem to be listening to and addressing my concerns? Is he or she cordial? Do I feel comfortable talking to that person?

These soft skills will literally make or break my impression of the doctor, and they'll determine whether or not I want to continue to give that person my business. Employers seek those same qualities that you may look for in a doctor.

This is, of course, not to diminish technical skills because they are important and integral to your success in your field. However, being the top of your class isn't going to cut it when you're competing against other professionals who were also the top of their class. Soft skills set successful people apart.

Technical skills may get you through the door — they may get you hired — but soft skills are what will make you advance.

Soft skills often get little respect or attention but, make no mistake, they will make or break your career.

## Successful People Have Mastered Soft Skills — And They Use Them

The most successful people I've encountered — mentors, superiors, people who are doing well in their lives and careers —all have great soft skills. Now, they may not be fluent in every aspect of every soft skill, but they have some strong suits in more than one of the soft skills areas. And it makes a huge difference for them.

I learned soft skills at an early age, due to my circumstances. I grew up in two different households. The house I called home was in a poor economic neighborhood. We struggled to make ends meet. But then on the weekends, I would typically be at my aunt's house, which was a middle class home. Growing up in a more urban setting, I felt like we had a team mentality in my home. We were struggling to survive, basically, and however anyone could contribute, he or she did. I got a job when I was twelve years old so that I could contribute. I learned how to communicate and problem solve in that environment. The environment itself demanded a certain type of personality — one that was willing to help, communicate, and be part of a team.

Then I'd go over to my auntie's house, and there was no struggle. People were living life instead of trying to survive to live life. However, I still needed my soft skills, just in a different way. There was still teamwork, a need for communication, and a need for emotional intelligence, but it was different. For me, I had to adapt to that new environment. I had to take on new communication methods, and I had to learn how to function just as well in that environment as I did in my home environment, which felt worlds away. I needed to be able to relate to people there who had struggles that were totally different than mine — struggles that I could have judged instead of relating to. I could have said, "You don't know what you're talking about - this isn't struggling!" but I wouldn't have been successful in that environment by doing so. Being empathetic to the fact that people had their own troubles, even if those troubles were less life and death than my own, meant that I was able to be a part of that community at my aunt's house. That was its own form of survival because my relationship to my aunt and the relationships I made in her world were ultimately really important to me.

So, what are these soft skills I'm talking about? Let's take a look at each one.

## Adaptability

Millennials by and large are the most flexible and adaptable group of people to hit the workforce. The freelance hub, Upwork, reported that millennials are 60% more adaptable than their Gen X counterparts.

The workplace demands adaptability. Organizations change directions, projects are modified, software is replaced, and the office culture can change under new management. Our society today is ever changing. Technology is old within five minutes. Being raised in an era of rapidly evolving technology and a seemingly infinite information flow - millennials are pretty accustomed to being flexible.

This ability to adapt well comes from this constantly changing world and is incredibly important in the corporate world. It can be easy to get used to one way of doing things or to get set on your vision for what "should" be happening. But being stuck and stubborn is not a way to align yourself for success.

About two years into my corporate career, my company underwent some reorganization and, as part of that, was eliminating some positions. Some people in my team were offered an opportunity to transition into the newer version of our team. I had a coworker who ultimately wasn't rolled into that team but was offered an opportunity to apply for other positions within the company. He wasn't fired; he just had to show some adaptability and show that he was willing and happy to work in a different capacity within the company. Instead, he pouted and refused to entertain the idea of doing anything but what he had signed up for. At that point, he was let go. Here was someone who could have had a great future within that company, but because they were asking him to do something that he hadn't anticipated, he totally shut down.

Co-workers, supervisors, processes, and approaches are constantly changing in the corporate world. If you are someone who gets flustered and demotivated by change occurring around you, you aren't going to be able to keep your head up and be as successful as you could be in the corporate world.

## Likability

Who is more likely to get hired? The savvy IT guy who can also conduct training sessions for new employees (because he is fun, relaxed, a good presenter, and a self-starter), or the savvy IT guy who keeps to himself and has trouble communicating with co-workers? A recent study showed that even when an employer disagrees with your point, if you are likable, they are more willing to entertain what you're suggesting. If you are less likable, they're more likely to disregard your –point — even if it is something valid. Interesting, huh?

Likability will take you to a lot of places, both personally and professionally. Being likable is one of the most — if not *the most* — significant soft skill one can possess. I once was on a company retreat at a resort in Cancun. We were at a karaoke event, and one of the CEOs suggested I get on stage and sing some songs by The Temptations. I was not interested! I'm the type of singer that doesn't sound good out of the shower. Plus, I had never done karaoke before. But, a few drinks later, he persisted, and I found myself on stage. The CEO loved it! He thought it was fantastic that I was brave enough to do it; plus, I was really entertaining once I was up there. I was interacting with the audience and everything.

He was so impressed that to my surprise, the CEO upgraded me to a Presidential Suite the next morning. That came 100% from him liking me. This was someone who was above me, but I was willing to mingle with him and show him my personality — and he liked it. If I had been closed off and antisocial none of that ever would have happened.

In addition to being socially available and open, a big component of likability is throwing away arrogance and replacing it with an embrace of others' accomplishments. Don't be so high and mighty about your own work that you aren't willing to pat someone else on the back. The workplace is largely about teamwork and a group effort toward a bigger purpose. Be part of that group mentality. Being part of the team and being there for your coworkers is a hugely important way to be indispensable to your company.

Contrary to what you might believe, likability isn't something you are born with. It's something you learn. Find common interests with people, be authentic, be compassionate, let out the crazy, and keep an open-mind.

## Communication

This is an area where millennials suffer in the corporate world. Effective communication — particularly proper verbal communication with management and peers — is something that millennials are reported time and time again as lacking in skill.

Part of the root of the issue is that millennials have trouble remembering that in life, as in the workplace, there is a pecking order. You might not like it, but your superior is your *boss*. He or she is in a position of power and demands the respect that holding that position deserves. Many millennials don't want to subscribe to the idea that their superiors are indeed *superiors* and want to live in a world where everyone is spoken to in a similar (read: casual) manner. That's a nice idea, but it's not reality. The people who are on the top tiers of power positions at major companies want to be treated as such.

As you know, non-verbal communication is on the rise, through text messaging, emailing, and social media. Since many people do indeed use a very casual communication style when using these forms of communication, it may give you a false perception that it's okay to talk at the office the same way you would via text messages. However, it's integral to understand that when communicating with a superior either verbally or non-verbally, respect and tact need to be employed.

I'll be the first to admit that I didn't possess proper communication skills when I started in the corporate world. I was lucky enough to have a mentor pull me aside and say, "Hey — your ideas are great, and you're doing great work, but when you write an email, you need to express yourself in a way that is more respectful to whom you're speaking to."

A few pointers for written communication:

1. When you join a company, pay attention to the tone that others use in emails to one another. There's a good chance that you'll be cc'd on a lot of inter-office communication. How do your contemporaries or people above you address the superiors in the office? How do the superiors address those who work below them? By paying attention to the written culture of the company,

you will learn the correct tone to use for your written communications.

2. Millennials have a poor reputation for having short attention spans. When you are responding to an email, make sure that you're addressing each question that was posed. Instead of making a speedy response your goal, make a thoughtful, full response your goal.

3. If a miscommunication or misunderstanding has occurred and a superior has questioned you about it via email, it can be tempting to write back immediately defending yourself. Instead, take a deep breath and make sure that you're giving yourself time to cool off to write a thoughtful response.

4. If you tend to ramble on in emails, work with a mentor or friend at figuring out how you can most effectively communicate in as few words as possible.

5. Don't use shorthand. LOL is not appropriate in a business-related email.

6. A few pointers for verbal communication:

7. Listen when spoken to, make eye contact when in conversation.

8. Be careful about using slang, and watch your tone. There is a way to speak to your peers, and there is a way to speak to your superiors.

9. It may sound simple, but it's really important to make sure that you're always being respectful! Approach all of your coworkers — peers and bosses alike — with respect. The workplace is a place of business and respect. Practice it!

## Problem Solving

Corporations care deeply that their employees be self-starters: people who can take an issue or a problem and come up with resolutions for that problem. Companies want people who can solve problems before they escalate to the higher-ups within the organization. The best type of problem solvers think on their feet and find creative solutions before a problem becomes a serious problem or issue.

Did you know that you can actually take classes online and earn certifications on problem solving? Learning Tree International offers a course in Critical Thinking and Problem Solving, and Georgia Tech offers an Advanced Problem Solving Certificate. If this is an area that gives you trouble, enrolling in one or both of these courses could be a huge benefit for you.

It can be really helpful to approach problems from a process point of view. Ask yourself:

1. What is the issue here?
2. What are some alternatives to solving this issue?
3. Consider the end result and process for each alternative solution. What will the outcome be? What will it take to get to that outcome?
4. Make sure that the solution is going to be beneficial. Sometimes we can find a solution to a problem that actually creates another problem down the road or just ultimately doesn't benefit the organization.

Employers like to see someone who has the ability to think on his or her feet, adapt to the situation, and think methodically about an issue. Problem solving will help you define your career.

## Be Open to Criticism

Here's what I say: "Criticism, shmiticism."

I've been criticized my whole career. Heck, I've been criticized my whole life. If you played a sport as a kid, you probably received some performance feedback. (Pointers on how to find more success with what you're doing.) Some people would call that criticism. Others would call it coaching (which is what it is).

Some criticism is just outright criticism, and it isn't constructive. Someone saying they don't like the color of your shirt, for example. If a piece of negativity directed at you is not constructive and doesn't have any intention of helping you in the future, then please, by all means, disregard it. Don't get invested or involved in that type of feedback — go ahead and call it criticism and shake it off.

Within the workplace, though, we often receive feedback that might sting the way criticism does, but since the feedback is designed to help you avoid making a similar mistake in the future, it shouldn't be disregarded. This type of feedback is actually aimed at helping you succeed — the same way your Little League coach was hoping to help you succeed when teaching you how to hold the bat.

What stands in the way of us shifting our perspective and accepting this feedback as coaching over criticism? Usually, it's our ego. We want to think that we knew what we were doing. But the truth is that anyone who has ever entered a career has needed to grow within it. And growing within a career is just the same as growing as a Little League player — you do your best, but there are people above you who are going to see things you're doing, and, based on their experiences, they're going to be able to give you tips and pointers about how you could be doing better, working more efficiently, and more successfully.

There's a famous story about Steve Kerr approaching Michael Jordan before the finals. Steve had noticed some things and wanted to share his observations because he thought they would be valuable going into the big game. He was scared to approach Michael Jordan, though, who was highly lauded as the best of the best. But Michael Jordan implemented every single one of Steve Kerr's criticisms. He didn't have an ego standing in his way — he just wanted to land at success, and he knew that taking Steve's observations to heart was the way to do that. He took responsibility for the fact that no one is perfect and everyone can always be improving — even if they're regarded as the best at what they do.

A lot of millennials don't want to hear advice from older people because we view the older generation as being behind the times. They don't use technology the way we do; they don't move at the pace we do; and they don't know what we do. Guess what? That is a hugely egotistical way to think. There is no universe in which experience doesn't garner you knowledge. As a millennial, you may need to fight your honest emotional response to disregard advice from someone whom you see as out of touch with your abilities and world. Take a step back and acknowledge where that person is coming from and remember he or she has succeeded in what you are working towards.

True managers are going to tell you things you don't want to hear because they are going to want to see you succeed. And let me tell you something — hearing things that you don't want to hear is going to sting! It always will. But you need to be aware of the emotions you're feeling, take a step back, and give that coaching an honest try.

Take the feedback and learn from it — it is the only way to grow, and growing is the only way to succeed.

## Growth & Shifting Perspective

Shifting perspective doesn't only work for overcoming criticism; it can absolutely be an asset when it comes to overcoming adversity. When you're hit with a stressful or seemingly impossible situation, don't just *react*. Try to practically work through it - how can you destress; how can you learn something from this confusing situation; how can you come out on top; how can you transform an annoying situation into a positive one? Asking yourself these questions will curb your impulses, prevent you from a negative reaction, and create a pathway for personal and professional growth. 'Cause lord knows, the roadway to success is a bumpy one with a lot of places to park, so keep your head in the game.

I have family members who can be totally crippled by adversity and who cannot see a situation as anything but negative and terrible. In order to rise above a situation, you need to be able to see the opportunity in it — whatever that is. Let's say your house burns down. That's terrible and tragic, and in the immediate days after it happens, you're going to feel really overwhelmed by what has befallen you. But in order to rise above it, a new perspective on that situation has to be born. At some point, you need to find inspiration and happiness in the prospect of finding a new home. You need to embrace the possibility in what you've been handed — the possibility to start anew. Yes, the initial circumstance was rattling. But what ultimately comes out of it needs to be something positive.

Shifting perspective has been incredibly important to me in my career and in my life. I, myself, have faced a lot of difficult situations where I have had to find a new perspective within them in order to carry on and ultimately rise above. I grew up in poverty, and I lost both of my parents at a young age. But although I've faced some big adversity in my own life, everything isn't as big as losing one's parents or one's house burning down. Sometimes it's your employer handing you a project at work that you really didn't want to be a part of, and now you're tasked with it, and you're feeling really overwhelmed and unhappy about it. You can let yourself feel those things, but if you want to succeed in your job, eventually, you're going to have to find a new perspective with which to approach that project. Look at it as an opportunity to be successful at something you thought was impossible, or a way to show your superiors that you're capable of overcoming challenges.

Finding a perspective that will help you be productive and, ultimately, successful is the best approach you can take in the workplace.

## Self-promotion

It's really important that you understand your worth. Most companies won't let you in on how valuable you are. It's important that you, yourself, are aware that the work you do is valuable.

One thing that I've always done is anytime I've earned an accolade, or a certification, or I've gotten a great evaluation from a manager or coworker, I record that new information into a portfolio that I can access anytime I need to express my worth. This way if I'm up for a promotion, I can go into the interview bolstered with the relevant certifications I've earned and verbiage from my performance reviews that support my fit for the position. Too many people in our generation think that they should be eligible for promotion without really having the facts to back up *why* they'd be right for that promotion. Going into a meeting about a promotion with hard evidence as to your success and dedication in your field helps you stand out amongst your peers.

A lot of people think that time worked is enough to get them a promotion, but that is not the case. The chances are that everyone who is going for the promotion will have also put in the time; they'll also have the degree, the experience, etc. You need to show what you can bring to the table that is specific to you and your success in that field. Successful projects you've worked on, praise from superiors, and real impact on the work that the organization is doing — these are the things that are going to get the attention of your superiors and really speak for your worth.

## Emotional Intelligence

Emotional intelligence is a skill that will benefit you in all aspects of your life, and it is a particularly strong skill to possess in the workplace. Emotional intelligence is basically your ability to read and understand the emotions, thought processes, and sensitivity of others, and to react and behave in a way that is congruent. It's your ability to read the temperature of a room and to behave appropriately to whatever is going on. For example, you should be able to tell when a coworker is getting worked up about something and rather than adding flames to the fire, you should behave in a way that ultimately calms the coworker down and boosts productivity.

Emotional intelligence makes your interactions with peers and superiors easier, and it is also an incredibly important skill for managers and superiors to have. From a management perspective, an employee who is aware of his or her subordinates' emotional limitations can coach and motivate those people through challenges, ultimately breeding success for the team.

There are a few different facets to overall emotional intelligence:

Self-awareness: Being aware of your own emotional state in a situation — how you're reacting in your gut and what associated emotions are appropriate to share and which you need to get under control yourself — is highly important in aligning yourself as a competent worker whom people want on their team.

Motivation: The ability to motivate yourself and others by recognizing the emotional roadblocks which surround a problem is a very attractive skill, particularly for those who have aspirations to move up in the ranks of a company.

Empathy: Empathy is highly regarded as one of the biggest building blocks of emotional intelligence. Being able to empathize with someone else means being able to put yourself in their shoes and understand how they're feeling, even though you aren't in the same situation that they're in. This is hugely important in the workplace, whether you're helping a peer through something difficult or motivating a subordinate to perform well under pressure.

Emotional intelligence is a really important social skill to possess, both in the workplace and outside of it.

## A Road Trip Worth Taking

Soft skills are portable, traveling with you wherever you go. They are externally influenced, relying heavily on the people who surround you, your circumstances, and life experience at large; and they exist on a lifelong continuum, meaning the journey to develop these skills is never-ending.

**Almost every successful person holds two thoughts to be true: the future can be better than the present, and I have the power to make it so.**

# Acquiring and Perfecting Soft Skills

## STEP 1: IDENITYFING SKILLS

*Go through each soft skill listed below and rate your skill ability 1-3. (with 1 being a strength and 3 being a weakness)*

_____ Adaptability

_____ Likability

_____ Communication

_____ Problem Solving

_____ Open to Criticism

_____ Ability to grow and shift perspective

_____ Ability to self-promote

_____ Emotional Intelligence

_____ Leadership

_____ Decision Making

_____ Time Management

_____ Ability to work well in a team

## STEP 2: COMPARE ANSWERS WITH ANOTHER PERSON

*Ask someone, who is trustworthy, to rate your soft skills using the same scale you did.*

_____ Adaptability

_____ Likability

_____ Communication

_____ Problem Solving

_____ Open to Criticism

_____Ability to grow and shift perspective

_____ Ability to self-promote

_____ Emotional Intelligence

_____ Leadership

_____ Decision Making

_____ Time Management

_____ Ability to work well in a team

*Compare your rating with his or her rating. Note: Sometimes you do know yourself better than others, so his or her answers are not necessarily truer than yours. However, it is interesting to see how others perceive you. If your person rated you differently on a specific skill, listen to what he or she has to say and determine whether you need to change your answer.*

## STEP 3: MAKE GOALS

*Pick one skill you rated a 3 and one skill you rated a 2 and make a specific goal and plan of action for how you will improve. List the skill you selected, make a specific goal, and then write down steps you need to take to meet the goal. See the example.*

*Example:*

*Skill I rated a 3: Time Management*

*Goal: Plan my time to maximize my work day and avoid multi-tasking.*

*Action Steps:*

1. *Write down what big projects need to be completed within the next month, and under each big project, break it into smaller tasks.*
2. *Write down what other things, besides the big*

   *projects, need to be done that month.*

3. *Every night for a month write down which tasks I will complete the next day and create a plan for the next day.*

4. *Follow my plan the next day at work.*

5. *At the end of the month, assess how well I did at managing my time. And start the process again for the next month.*

Skill I rated a 3:_____

Goal:_____

Action steps to meet the goal:

_____

_____

_____

Skill I rated a 2:_____

Goal:_____

Action steps to meet the goal:

_____

_____

_____

# CHAPTER 6

---~---

# INCREASE YOUR VALUE

When I first entered corporate America, I had one big interest. MONEY. I admit that openly. I was focused on the money.

Many millennials are focused on getting jobs that will generate enough income that they feel comfortable and happy doing the things they want to do. Of course this makes sense — money will always be a part of the career equation. However, once you get a job and the paychecks start rolling in, shift your focus. Keep your professional goals at the forefront. Building a career is not just about that paycheck — it's about owning your future success by staying focused on growth and potential. It's easy to get stuck focusing on the ins and outs of your current position, but it's important that you continue to think about how your actions fit into your overall goals. Treat the big picture of your career as though it is its own business. Be the CEO of your career. As the CEO of the entity that is your career, you need to make smart business decisions that will foster growth.

When you're applying for jobs, the struggle to get your foot in the door is real. But — and I know you might not want to hear this — once that foot is in the door, that's when the true struggle begins! Don't sit comfortably at your new desk and figure that since you've arrived, you're done. The truth is that this is just the beginning. Now, it's time to look at what type of resources you have available to you so that you can get the training you need to advance your skills and become increasingly valuable to your company.

Big companies offer a *ton* of opportunity to enhance your skill set. A lot of big companies also offer office culture perks like table tennis and free food. While those fun benefits may be easy to focus on, don't turn a blind eye to the skill set opportunities that are also available to you.

Trust me: increasing your value by adding to your skill sets is how you will achieve the goals you set out for yourself.

## Learn From my Mistakes

The first major company I worked for offered a ton of resources. They offered certifications that I needed. They offered workshops. They offered foreign language training so that I could be equipped to take on overseas work. They offered a ton of opportunities to add skills to my resume that I needed down the road in order to advance in my career — all of free!

Guess how many of these benefits I took advantage of?

*None.*

It pains me to even write it out! I can't believe how blind I was to the amazing potential that existed in all of these benefits that were offered to me.

A few years later, the contract I was working on was terminated. Within my company, if your contract ended and you didn't have another contract to move onto immediately, you were "put on the bench." Basically, you were put in an employment holding, where you waited until you had another contract offer. If two months passed and you hadn't been eligible for a contract, the company considered letting you go because they deem you unmarketable for enough contracts to be considered a valuable employee.

While I was "on the bench," a bunch of contracts came up requiring skills that I didn't have. Certain certifications. Attendance at certain workshops. Foreign language skills. These were all skills that I could have possessed if I had taken advantage of the company's earlier offers, but I hadn't. As a result, those contracts were getting filled by my colleagues, and there I was sitting on the bench.

Eventually, I ended up getting cut. I wasn't marketable enough, which is mind boggling because while I was on the bench, if I could have taken my head out of the sand, I could have taken advantage of resources at that point! But I was so focused on getting my next contract and worrying about my next check that I totally overlooked the fact that the answer was staring me straight in the face in the form of resources offered by my company.

After I was let go, I had to use the last little bit of money that I had left to take a course that would qualify me for more competitive contracts — a class that my previous company would have paid for had I taken it then. With that course under my belt, I applied for a job and got hired right away. I've never looked back, and I've never stopped taking advantage of the resources available to me.

## What are Company Resources?

Google is well-known for its campus, which is stocked with company resources like in-house catering, retreats for employees, and a dog-friendly atmosphere. Unfortunately, not *every* company is going to take a page out of Google's playbook. You may not be able to bring your dog to work, or have an all-expenses paid trip to a company workshop and retreat — but what you *do* have available may actually surprise you. Companies are beginning to understand the importance of making their employees happy.

In her book, *Make More Money by Making Your Employees Happy*, Dr. Noelle Nelson, a clinical psychologist, says, "When employees feel that the company takes their interest to heart, then the employees will take company interests to heart." She's got a point. Happiness does often breed loyalty.

But beyond creating an atmosphere of satisfaction, companies are starting to realize that they can make amenities available to their employees which actually boost the employee's value, such as workshops and other professional advancement opportunities.

**Company resources intersect the organization's goals and plans with the goals and plans of the employee.** Organizations offer these services to their employees to promote an environment of growth, both on the company and individual level. So, what kind of things do companies traditionally offer?

**Workshops.**
Companies will often offer optional workshops. When I was starting out and didn't realize how much attending a workshop could add value to my portfolio, I totally used to blow these things off. Not mandatory? Not going.

I was *completely* overlooking the value of attending a workshop. Workshops are great places to meet people. They also work to enhance your skills and introduce you to new ideas that diversify your work palette.

Typically workshops are geared toward career advancement and knowledge growth inside a particular field of work. So, if you work at a marketing firm, you may have a workshop like *Digital Marketing Strategy Building* or *How to Create and Manage a Content Library.*

It's in your best interest to soak up as much as you can since these resources are geared toward you specifically, and they are usually *free.* Plus, adding new skills to your repertoire will enhance your marketability.

It's important to remember to go into a workshop with an open mind. There is an extremely good chance that you're going to learn something you didn't expect to learn. Go in with an open mind and see what the workshop has to offer.

**Team Building Activities.**
Volunteering, outdoorsy trips, cook-offs, and other company-wide events can help strengthen soft skills like interpersonal relationships, problem solving, and adaptability. Best of all? They level the playing field for company bigwigs and all the rest of us. Imagine going indoor rock climbing with your company. The CEO is the one climbing the wall, and you're the one holding the support rope. Not only does this require the CEO to acknowledge your

existence (which in some organizations can be a daunting task), but he or she is also putting his or her trust in you. That's a great way to build a relationship that lets your superiors think of you as a person and an integral part of the team. Now, you have a connection you wouldn't have had otherwise, and you can impart a great lasting impression. A networking win for sure.

In addition to team building activities with a company, a lot of bigger companies are now doing informal, fun challenges where one company competes against another company in a sport or other event. These types of events are a really fun way to meet people from other companies, which is, of course, great for networking.

**Tuition Reimbursement.**
Some companies will actually support you financially if you decide to go to school to pursue a degree that will make you eligible for a higher position within the company. This is a way for a company to essentially invest in a future with you.

Most companies who offer this benefit offer it on the contingency that you stay with the company for a specified amount of years after receiving the degree since they are footing the bill for the degree. Some people feel put off by the idea of a time commitment because they don't want to be locked down. You know what I say to a time commitment? *So what!* The company is paying for the education, which will make you valuable to other companies as well. It's not as though you're going to advance to a position that requires that degree without it — regardless of what company you're at.

This is a benefit you should absolutely take advantage of if it is offered to you. It shows dedication to the pursuit of higher positions within the company, and, ultimately, it is a huge boost to your value — within the company that's paying for it and beyond. Always think about the big picture. Staying with a company a little longer and leaving with a degree that makes you valuable to the market at large is absolutely a good strategic move. Understand the investment that you're making by taking on a tuition reimbursement arrangement and the positive value that investment can have on your future.

**Management Training Programs.**
In-house promotion is happening more and more as employers are preferring to retrain, or cross-train, an existing employee rather than hiring someone new. This practice rewards existing employees for their hard work, and it cultivates an environment of trust and encouragement.

To that end, many companies offer management-training programs. Every company has specific ways that they want things run. Those preferences change company to company. Management training programs are geared toward explaining how to be a leader within the confines of the preferences of a specific company.

If you've got your sights set on moving up the career ladder, investing your time and energy in a management-training program will help you get your foot in the door. Management programs teach you how to be a leader, how to take educated risks, how to have autonomy in decision-making, and how to delegate and manage a team; all skills that will serve you throughout both your professional and personal life.

## Skill Specific Certifications.

Like management training programs, companies see a desire from employees to advance their skills, and employers see a growing need to provide an arena for this to happen. Certification programs focus on individual skill sets (for example, you can take a certification program on boosting your soft skills).

The certificates you gain in a certification program are granted by external organizations and are yours to keep - forever. So not only are you making a solid impression within your current company, you're also adding to your resume and increasing your value overall.

## Fitness Classes.

A lot of organizations will offer discounts on gym memberships (and will even allow you to take a longer lunch break if you're going to work out!). Other companies actually provide fitness classes on site like zumba, yoga, and self-defense classes to encourage employees to lead a healthy lifestyle. This is a great opportunity for you to get in shape - which is shown to be a habit of successful people - and a chance to get to know your co-workers a little better.

Healthy living — fitness, nutrition, et al — can actually hugely benefit your career. It gives you a sense of grounding in your life, and it gives you energy to do your work to the best of your ability. If you company is offering support in the pursuit of healthy living, it's a great idea to take advantage of that benefit.

## Company Perks.

Less traditional company resources known as perks are catered toward a lively and creative workforce (read: millennial). Remember Google? Perks like time off incentives, company retreats, work-from-home options, work-sponsored catering, freebies, and even office game rooms are becoming the norm in corporate office culture.

And while company resources and employee perks are different, they serve a similar purpose: to transform you into a happier, more creative, knowledgeable and motivated person. A happy person is a productive person. The more productive you are, the more you will increase your competitive advantage, the easier you'll rise in the ranks, and the **more likely you'll have the tools to carve out the future you've always dreamt of.**

# Company Resources Inventory

## STEP 1: ASSESS COMPANY RESOURCES

*Make a list of all the resources your company offers. You may need to contact your human resource department and/or manager.*

_____

_____

_____

_____

_____

_____

## STEP 2: MAKE A PLAN TO UTILIZE RESOURCES

*Determine which resources you should utilize and plan your action steps and timeline for each resource.*

*Example: I want to be a project manager*

- *Enroll in the company funded PMP class (3 month class)*

# THE MILLENNIAL TAKEOVER

- *Attend leadership workshops (5 day workshop)*
- *Shadow and work with other project managers (6 months)*

_____

_____

_____

_____

_____

_____

_____

_____

_____

_____

_____

# CHAPTER 7

$\sim$

# MENTORS: A LIFELINE FOR MILLENNIAL CAREER SUCCESS

Many millennials believe that just by having *gone to college,* they are equipped to be the CEO of a company. Not every millennial thinks this way, but unfortunately, you will find a number of people among your ranks that feel that they've already "put in their time" by merely attending college.

This, of course, is very off base. In fact, you can't really start putting in your time until you are out of college and in the workplace. Once you are in the workplace, you have a lot to learn. One of the best ways to learn is from someone who is more experienced than yourself. Someone who is wise and who can advise you on what actions you can take to successfully achieve the things that he or she has achieved thus far in his or her career. This is where a mentor can have a huge impact on your career.

A mentor is someone who has walked down the path you're walking down right now. Since he or she has been in your shoes, he or she can easily see things about yourself and what you're doing that you might not be able to see yourself. It can be really hard to have perspective on your own actions because you're in your skin. A mentor is someone who can be honest with you and — if you listen to his or her wisdom — can really help you on your path toward achieving your goals.

A mentor is someone you want in your corner. This mentor can help you "grow up" professionally by sharing his or her experiences and perspectives on what you're going through, and by giving you advice on how to deal with obstacles that come up in your journey.

## My Mentor

I entered corporate America straight from the military. Prior to that, I had grown up in the inner-city. I was an urban youth. Interestingly, there are some commonalities between the military and growing up in an urban environment. In both of those realities, the communication style is very direct. If you have an issue, it is addressed bluntly and forwardly. When you get into corporate America, though, you can't exactly call people out on everything you see and expect that to fly. You have to be a little bit more careful and tactful with how you address people, how you handle issues, and how you present yourself in a range of situations.

When I first entered the scene, the way that I responded to emails was, well, terrible. I didn't realize that I couldn't be blunt and direct —my emails sounded rude and dismissive. My written communications didn't have any finesse or grace. I was just saying what I thought and firing emails off — to peers, to superiors, to everyone.

One day, a woman in my office pulled me aside and said that she thought I was a great guy, and she wondered if I could I could help her out. Her son was part of a program in which he needed a mentor, and she wondered if I could mentor him. She said that in turn, she would mentor me and help me with the things she saw I needed help with in my new corporate reality.

I don't mind admitting that in that moment, I almost told her no! I thought I was doing just fine. My ego was there patting me on the back, telling me that I was perfect in everything I was doing. The truth was that at that moment, I was on my way out. They were about to get rid of me. I didn't fit! I didn't fit into the culture that was surrounding me. I didn't know how to present myself or how to behave properly within the rules of the game. I was likable — I just didn't fit.

I'm so glad to say that I didn't turn that offer of mentorship away. Instead, I started meeting with her daily. She helped me with so many aspects of my day to day operations that I had no idea I needed help with. She corrected my grammar because my written communication was all over the place. She helped me figure out how to *effectively communicate.* She taught me how to correspond properly, driving home the importance of being clear and concise while also being polite and professional. She completely turned around the way that I communicated within the workplace, and honestly, I think she saved my career.

At the same time that I was working with this mentor, I was receiving advice and support from another person at my office. As a manager of my department, he was two or three years down the road from where I stood. One day we were at a corporate event, and I told him that I wished I could learn from his experiences so that I could one day be where he was in his career. He said, "Oh, like a mentorship?" I said yes! That was exactly what I was hoping for. He agreed instantly.

So while I had a mentor showing me how to be professional and how to behave within the professional world, this second mentor taught me how to advance professionally. What moves did I need to make in order to get myself to the next level, and then the next, and the next? He taught me to be proactive. For example, rather than wait for my manager to request a meeting with me, he advised me to ask the manager directly for a meeting so that I could get feedback. He advised me on questions to ask. He taught me how to look at the other positions available above me and to delineate what skills I would need to acquire and hone before I could consider myself eligible for those positions.

If it weren't for these two mentors, I would not be where I am today. They taught me how to survive and how to advance — the two biggest necessary skills for thriving in one's career.

## Why Mentors are Important

A mentor acts as your guiding light — a crutch to rest on if you're feeling a bit worn down, and a sounding board as you navigate your future professional life. As a go-getter, you can sometimes get wrapped up in all of the excitement of being your own boss, or designing a career path that aligns with your values and professional goals. Getting sidetracked and bombarded with information is super easy in the digital age. A mentor can help streamline some of the chaos and help keep you focused.

Contrary to traditional networking –situations — where you may toss a business card or two at someone and never hear from them again — mentors will be there with you for the long haul. They invest in your future, and to do so, they invest their time, resources, and energy to ensure you become the most successful person you can be. These are good relationships to have.

Some mentors may establish a long-term commitment to you that involves weekly meetups to discuss the wins and woes of the week, career advice, personal strength and weakness assessments, future training opportunities, and community networking engagements. Other mentorships may be for a concentrated but shorter amount of time such as a week or a month. Others still are less formal and evolve naturally over time.

It's not unusual for mentors to play larger roles in your life. Mentors offer you emotional support as you work your way through the ups and downs of establishing a career, and they advise you on smart decision making in the workplace. A good mentor can talk your head out of the sand when you've gotten stuck and can influence how you behave in and react to different situations within the workplace. Often, mentors and mentees build a bond that lasts years beyond when the mentee reaches the goal he or she set out to achieve under the watchful eye of the mentor. However, one of the major benefits of a mentor is that he or she is not your *friend*. A mentor is almost like a Career Parent. It's someone who can be honest with you, can give you tough love when you need it, and who wants to see you succeed to the point where, ultimately, you'll thrive without him or her by your side.

Research suggests that people who hang around a mentor tend to see a higher salary in addition to vocational and psychosocial help. And, another study shows that early career professionals show higher subjective career success than those who don't have mentors. Where productivity is high, so is career success — and productivity is often born from a mentor/mentee relationship. So, how's that for incentive?

Of course not all mentors are cut from the same cloth so take your time finding the right one for you.

## How To Find a Mentor

You may have your career vision sights set high, and that's great. However, it's crucial that you set smaller goals as you strive to conquer the bigger ones. Why? Because if you want to be the director of an international media agency (or something thereabouts), you must achieve smaller goals along the way. It's beneficial to draw up a three year roadmap to career success. The end of these three years does not have to be your final destination: it's more like a rest stop a few hours in on a cross-country road trip.

This rest stop is necessary in order for you to complete your larger goal. I mean, you wouldn't be able to drive 3,000 miles without stopping for gas, a bathroom break, or a little sleep, would you?

As part of your three year plan picture, I advise you to find a mentor who is about three years ahead of where you are today. He or she will have relevant and accurate information to impart to you about your current journey. It's fine to work with someone who is further down the road than three years, but I've found that many of the most effective mentorship relationships have that smaller window between the now and the then.

And find the *best one*. Don't just go out and pick someone you're friendly with and feel comfortable talking to and slap the name mentor on him or her. The qualifications for a mentor should be someone who has insight on the path you need to take in order to achieve the goals you want to achieve. This doesn't necessarily mean working with someone who has the exact position you want down to the road. Actually, it can be helpful to work with someone who is within your company but works for a different department. Working with someone who works for a different company can bring perspective, too. However, if you do work with someone from another company, just be sure that he or she is in a similar position to where you want to land so that the language is the same.

It's really all about figuring out what it is you need to learn at this stage in your career and who can help you the most in that pursuit. It's possible that you may need different mentors for different aspects of your career, or that you might need different mentors at different stages of your life and career. That's fine! As you advance towards your career goals, you can begin seeking out mentors who are closer and closer to your own final destination.

A couple of other things to note:

**Know what you're looking for.**
Serendipity plays a role sometimes, but most of the time, the perfect mentor isn't about to walk up to you on the street, shake your hand, and reveal him or herself to be your mentor soulmate. Instead of expecting fate to take over, dig deep and figure out *why* you want a mentor and *what* you're trying to get out of the relationship. Do you want to use them for networking? Or, would you rather receive career advice and guidance? Once you're clear what you want your mentor to help you learn or achieve, you can evaluate who might be available to help you on this journey.

**Look to your community.**
Mentors don't have to be limited to people in your office space. Look around at your alma mater, other

colleges, non-profit organizations, churches, community organizations and within your family and friend group. You can also jump online and check out SCORE mentors (www.score.org/mentors) to find an online career mentor. Someone willing to help you out may be right under your nose, but you'll never know if you don't ask.

**Get together.**
Once you've found someone who fits the bill in terms of what you need from a mentor, carve out some time for you and he or she to sit down and discuss the mentorship. What type of a time commitment is the mentor willing to offer to you? What expectations does the mentor have of you? What types of accomplishments will he or she expect you to achieve in order to continue being mentored?

**Be Respectful.**
Remember — a mentorship is all about benefiting your career, and someone else is dedicating his or her precious time to that goal. When you're with your mentor, turn off your cell phone and forget about social media. Treat every minute that you are in your mentor's presence as an opportunity to learn and grow.

# Questions To Ask Your Mentor

What if I were to ask you the following question: *Did you have a good day?*

Chances are you would end up responding with, "It was great," and then the conversation would hit a dead end. These are called yes-no questions, and they should be avoided at all costs when dealing with a mentor.

If I changed the wording to: *What was something that made you feel accomplished today?* You would be forced to expand your answer a bit. See what happened there?

Having a mentor is a two-way street: you get out what you put in. Mentors exist to help you, but they can only help you if you know what you need help with. Plan to ask your mentor plenty of questions, and come to meetings with your mentor prepared with questions to ask.

Craft your questions to be thoughtful, specific, and to evoke a detailed and equally thoughtful answer. You should focus on questions that someone who is three years ahead of you can look back and answer with perspective.

Some examples might include:

- What did you do differently than your peers to bring your where you are today?
- What are three things you wish you would have known at my stage?
- How did you define "success" when you were starting out?
- What sort of potholes did you hit on your journey and how did you resolve them?
- What was your biggest weakness? How did you strengthen it?
- If you could do one thing differently, what would it be and why?

These are a few examples that can open up a rich and informative dialogue with your mentor. Also don't be afraid to establish a rapport with him or her by asking about his or her family, hobbies, passions, and the kicker - what you can do to help them.

Most mentors figure that the mentee - you - is concerned only with taking. Show the mentor you're different and you're interested in him or her as a person, not just a career professional. Doing this will also allow you to feel like you have a better understanding of how your mentor got to this advanced position and how you can deepen your relationship with him or her.

A mentor empowers you to see a possible future, and to believe it can be obtained.

## Beyond Mentors

In addition to learning from someone in your own physical world, there is a lot to be learned by reading books, blogs, and tweets written by someone you look up to or who has had experiences that could benefit your journey. Although reading the wisdom of people you don't know isn't as interactive as a mentorship, their experiences can nevertheless add to your arsenal of knowledge.

One of my mentors is Tony Robbins. Have I ever met Tony Robbins? No! But I've read every single thing he's written, and I've related everything I've read to my own experiences. I've taken advice from what he's written and I've applied it to my own career, and I think my career is better off for it.

You also need to learn how to act as your own mentor. Learn how to take a step back and evaluate your own performance. Be as brutally honest with yourself as a mentor would be with you were he or she present. By becoming more objectively aware of yourself and your limitations, you can begin to act as a check for your own actions.

## Mentor Questionnaire

1. What do you want your mentor to help you achieve? (Examples: marketing yourself, getting a promotion, networking, career advice etc.)

_____

_____

_____

2. Who in your field is 3 years ahead of where you are and has experience in the aspect you want to work on? (Remember this can be someone in your own company or someone in another company, but remember he or she should be in a similar position. You can list more than one possibility. )

_____

_____

_____

3.  What questions can you ask your mentor in that initial meeting, so he/she knows what you need/want help with?

_____

_____

_____

# CHAPTER 8

~

# MILLENNIAL CAREER BRANDING WILL USHER IN SUCCESS

There was a time when someone trying to get a job made it his or her goal to impress the employer during an interview, using calculated answers to standardized questions. Guess what? Those days are gone.

Today, an employer often vets you as a person before you even step foot in the door. How? Social media. Most millennials are visible on social media. The culmination of your tweets, Facebook posts, Instagram shots, and LinkedIn profile make up your career brand, whether you realize it or not. The opinions you share and the experiences you broadcast say a lot about who you are, what your interests are, and what type of a personality you have. And trust me — prospective employers are checking your online profile out.

This is not just something I'm saying. I've personally spoken to HR reps at some of the biggest companies in –the US — Hallmark, HR Block, DST Solutions — and they have all told me that the first thing they do when they receive a resume for an open vacancy is review candidates' social media profiles. Your social media contributes to your personal brand and gives the potential employer a snapshot of your image. Potential employers want to know whether the image you portray will fit with their corporate brand, and social media is a first impression of that. With that in mind, be smart. Filter your posts. As fun as Facebook (and other platforms) can be - tone it down. Would you walk into an interview and start discussing last weekend's shenanigans? Sharing party posts or inappropriate memes will haunt you. If you want to be serious about developing a professional career brand, quit posting things that don't reflect that notion. Warren Buffett once said, "It takes 20 years to build a reputation and only five minutes to ruin one." Be wise.

There's an old adage that I myself use a lot — dress for the job you want, not the job you have. Present yourself in such a way where you fit the bill for the position that's three years ahead of yours. You have to do this on social media and in person — in the way you dress, in the way you present yourself in written and verbal communications, and in the way you act within the team and in the workplace (and in some cases, how you act outside of the workplace). If you want a promotion down the road, you need to present yourself as though you would be an asset (not a liability) if you were you to hold that position within the company.

When you are hired for a position within a company, you're expected to fit the role that the position requires. For many companies, that means not being overly controversial, not displaying any lewd or illegal behavior, and basically being an all around respectable, easy to approach person. There was a time when you could act like a model employee at work yet still do and say whatever you wanted at home; however, smartphones and social media completely changed the game.

## What is a Career Brand?

*You* are your career brand. And yes, you already have one.

The term *branding* is not a new concept. Farmers brand their cattle to distinguish them from others. Likewise, companies began to brand themselves using logos, value content, product uniqueness and names that distinguish them from other businesses. A brand is a cultural identity that sets one product or company apart from another. It's how we identify who or what something is and what that group or individual stands for.

Your career brand is individual to you, and it is defined by a culmination of your resume — your accolades — your online presence, the way that you present yourself, and ultimately, the way you act within the workplace. Your brand is a reflection of who you are as a person and as a professional. It's what makes you tick, what ticks you off, what you're willing to work hard toward and stand behind. It's your image — how you present yourself. What people know about you before they even meet you. It's the story you tell the world about who you are, what you do, and how you handle yourself. And it can be a key ingredient to advancing your career, if you're mindful of the story you're telling and how it fits into the big picture of the company you're working for.

The online aspect of your brand largely comes in to play when you're going through the job seeking process. The reason we look up restaurants, hotels, tourist destinations, and events online before we commit to going to them is the same reason human resources managers look people up online before deciding whether or not to interview or hire them. It's a feature of the times we live in.

Let's give this a try. Put down this book for a moment and go to the computer and Google your name (and your town if your name is more common). What do you see? Check out the results that come back. Swim through the information one gets when doing a quick search of your name. These results are the same bits of information that a future - or current - employer will see. When your resume is sitting on the desk of a human resources manager, and he or she is trying to decide who to bring in for an interview (or who to cut), this is what they're going to see. Do those Google results speak to who you are? Are you proud of what shows up?

Based on what you see there, would you hire you?

I actually had an experience where my social media infringed on my own professional life. A few years back, I was aware that Facebook was a place employers were looking to vet hopefuls, but for whatever reason, I thought Twitter was a safe place to go all out. I wasn't being terribly crazy, but I was retweeting things that I found amusing, some of which would not be considered appropriate fodder for the professional world. Well, I interviewed for a position that I didn't get, which I didn't think too much of at the –time — I just figured hey, it happens. But then a recruiter from the same company was discussing a position with me later in that same year. Clearly, the company thought a lot of my accolades, so I decided to ask the recruiter why I hadn't been picked the first time around. She did some digging and found out that the company had seen my Twitter account, and they didn't feel like I was representing myself in a way that was in line with the company's values. I was shocked! I promptly went back in and cleaned up my Twitter account, and I've kept it clean since. It's never been a problem again.

As we have established, the question is not whether or not you have a brand. You invariably have one. The question is: how can you manage the elements that make up your brand so that your brand is working for you? How can you present yourself in the most professional fashion? How can you populate your social media feed so that if a potential employer browses it, they see something that is in line with who you are and how good a fit you would be for their company? How can you show that you're a team player and that you'd be an asset in the workplace?

Shama Hyder, whom Fast Company proclaimed "Millennial Master of the Universe," concludes, "The question is no longer IF you have a personal brand, but if you choose to guide and cultivate the brand or to let it be defined on your behalf."

So, let's look at how we can hone your brand so that it's working for you, not against you.

## Brand Consistency

Millennials joining the workforce have to rely heavily on soft skills to make up for where their experience lacks. A career brand backs you up where your resume fails you, and it can shine light on characteristics you possess that aren't quantifiable but are absolutely desirable. A career brand highlights what is distinct about you, and it's pivotal for the advancement of your career and your mark on the world. It's the most vital tool you have in your toolbox and every successful career professional you know - and don't know - has cultivated it.

The professional world is fast paced, and there isn't much room for missteps. Therefore, before making a hiring decision, companies spend a good amount of time vetting the people whom they are considering bringing on board. These first impressions will be formed based on how they feel about your overall image. Your social media *plays a pivotal part in* this. A lot of millennials feel like this is unjust, or that it unfairly stacks the odds against you. Is it unjust? I don't know. But what I do know is that it's happening every day. So you should plan for it and figure out how to make sure it's working for you. You want to make sure you are perceived as a career professional.

Look at Oprah Winfrey, Jon Stewart, Jay Z or Beyonce; they are all prime examples of the embodiment of a brand. They are thought-leaders, pioneers, professionals in their industries. If you take a look at their social media or their public appearances, their behavior supports the brands that they have established for themselves. They are careful to be sure that the media (social or otherwise) they can control about themselves is in line with their values.

You may not be a celebrity, but continuity across your brand is just as important for your career as it is for their careers. Most employers will have the gist of who you are from your digital brand before you even walk through the door. Maintaining this image during the interview, after you're hired, and as you progress to new and exciting things is just as important as crafting your career brand to begin with.

Many may view this as me telling you to not be authentic or to sell out, but you should throw those terms out the door when dealing with your professional image. You have to act according to the role that you have decided best aligns with what you want *and how you want to grow in your career.* If you are striving to have a career life that is in line with who you are, this really shouldn't be a problem. Remember that authenticity is key. Don't force something you're not: your career brand should reflect you as a person, not a pseudo-self. The Harvard Business Review found that 64% of people have a relationship with a brand because of shared values. Stick true to you and the rest will follow.

Living your brand really boils down to being accountable and having a heightened self-awareness. For example, I work as a consultant. In the healthcare field, I have multiple clients. As a coach, I have multiple clients. When people are looking to hire me or to work with me, the first thing they do is Google me. I know this because I ask clients, and they tell me! So, they Google me, and they basically do an extensive background check on who I am, how I sound, and what I talk about.

Before they even bring me through the door — before they even contact me — they want to know who I am. They want to know if I'm reputable, and they want to know if the things I talk about on social media are in line with the things I promote about myself as a professional. As a consultant and a career coach, if you went to my Twitter, and it was all about my crazy exploits on trips to Cabo, you'd think twice about my advice here — especially about branding and social media awareness! I know that, so I've worked hard to make sure that anything I put out into the world is consistent with what I preach.

**Think of yourself as a brand.**
Change your perspective and start thinking of yourself as the CEO. You are the CEO of your career. How you manage your career — how you elevate your career, the skills you obtain, the accomplishments, the accolades, how you position yourself — think of it all as business decisions you're making as CEO of your career.

If you owned a company, you most likely wouldn't show up to the office hung over, and you wouldn't invite all of your subordinates out for pancakes with you so that you could drool into that plate of pancakes looking like the world has just ended. As the CEO of your own company, your career, you shouldn't be inviting the world to those experiences either. You have your bad days, but that doesn't mean you have to put them front and center of your public persona.

**Make your brand exceptional.**

As CEO of your career, strive to make your brand the top of the line — the brand that the other brands wish they were. Be the Apple. Be the brand that people know they can expect greatness from.

How do you make sure that your brand is top notch? Image control, which I addressed earlier, is important. Equally important is making sure that you are bolstering yourself with the certifications and the soft skills to make you stand out in the crowd. You want to be known for reliability. If a higher up in your company says they need someone with X skill to take on a new project, you want to be the person who everyone says, "I bet ___ can take that on and do a great job at it."

Be the standard. Make sure you look like a star player. Perform at a high level, achieve at a high level, and make sure that you represent yourself as the high achiever that you are. In that, it's also important to associate with strong brands. If you're a brand, so is everyone else in your company. A corporation isn't going to align themselves with someone whose values don't line up with theirs, and neither should you! Instead, align yourself with likeminded people who are headed the same direction you are. Find the people in your workplace or in your field who have established themselves as responsible, reliable achievers, and earn their respect. Respect from those people will speak volumes for your brand.

## Branding Tips to Help you Land (and Keep) the Job

Ask yourself, what makes you important? Why do you do the things you do? How do you stand out from the other 493 people vying for the job you want? What is your value proposition? Why should they choose you over the next person?

**Take stock of your accomplishments.**
Continue to add to your tool belt and make yourself more valuable. Build a reservoir of professional successes that will lay the foundation for your career brand. Your unique accomplishments will give you the competitive edge you need to get that promotion or land that job. Direct your energy towards enhancing your education through certifications, taking on more challenging work,

volunteering, and doing things that will only make you more valuable to a future employer.

Some credentials cost money, and often, earning those certifications is a wise investment in your future within your career. There are also ways to add to your value that don't cost any money. For example, volunteering. Volunteering will enhance your soft skills, will illustrate that you are a team player, and will help you make connections — and it won't cost you a thing. Shadowing individuals on your team is another non-financial way to boost your value and your store of knowledge, as is independently studying a subject so that you become a subject matter expert.

**Nurture your image.**
Three words: dress for success.

As much as you may have been told otherwise, appearance *does* matter. There's an old adage that says dress for the job you want to get. Understand the role and the place that you're in. If you show up for an interview at a corporate job wearing Birkenstocks and shorts, you will stick out like a sore thumb. Find out what attire is considered appropriate for the workplace you're entering and dress accordingly.

Not only does the way you present yourself make a difference, but the way you carry yourself does too. You may look the part, but can you communicate and use appropriate soft skills to secure an opportunity? Make sure that you're up on current business etiquette. How are you expected to behave around peers, and how are you expected to behave around superiors? For example, a man holding a door for a woman is considered polite; however, in certain workplaces, a man holding the door for a woman could imply that the woman is inferior to the man. Even though it might go against your instincts in terms of politeness, there could be politics and in-business politeness at play. Take stock of what's going on around you, and do your best to behave within the culture of the company you're at.

Confidence is also part of image. You want to appear confident in your abilities. Make sure that when you're in the workplace, you are calm and confident. Second guessing yourself or being too self-deprecating can create the wrong image.

**Don't let your guard down.**
I worked at a big corporate company that offered a thing called "Beer Fridays." Basically, every Friday, the company would have a big social event where drinks were served. For the most part, people had

one or maybe two –drinks — the idea was to be casual and social, but not to be drunk. Well, there was one guy in my company who figured hey, free booze — I'm going to make the most of it. This became a pattern. Every week, he would drink way more than everyone else. He was the life of the party, and we all had fun with him, but ultimately the higher ups in the company took notice and started to feel like he wasn't a good fit for the overall culture of the company. Because he wasn't keeping himself in check at those –events — which although they were social were still nevertheless a work –event — it highlighted the fact that he was not on the same wavelength as everyone else in the company. It wasn't long before he was let go.

It's important to make sure you are aware of how you're coming off at all work-related events, whether it's deemed "social" or not. It all falls under the general umbrella of your image and your brand.

**Contribute to the conversation.**
Your voice matters. Engage people online to enhance your brand and to create a clear picture of your perspectives, ideas, and thought-processes. Craft a voice that represents you and your professionalism as a whole. Showcase yourself as a thought-leader. For the first half of my career, I spent a lot of time being quiet in conversations

where my opinion would have mattered a whole lot. I, ultimately, could have saved my company time and money if I had shared what I was thinking, which would have proved my value. I lacked the confidence to realize that my thoughts were worthwhile and could actually help.

At the same time, it's really important to have awareness of what's going on around you and to know your place. Sometimes you're going to be in a room with two people who are more experienced than you, and they are going to have a back and forth about something that you don't necessarily have a lot to contribute on. That's okay. Just sit and listen and learn from the exchange you're lucky enough to witness. Don't be so focused on boosting your own brand that you're interjecting when it would be better if you didn't.

Also, be aware of when and where it is appropriate to engage in certain conversations, and behave accordingly. Is Twitter really the best place to get into a deep debate with a family member? Maybe, but maybe having that conversation offline would better serve your image.

**Develop an elevator pitch.**
Can you explain what you do, where you're going, and why in 30 seconds or less? If not, it's time to

start working on a quick and to-the-point answer to the question: so, what do you do? If you can nail this pitch, it will show people you're focus is clear, you're committed, and you'll find more doors opening for you.

In my career, I worked at a corporation where if you ended up in the elevator with the CEO, he wanted you to tell him what you did at the company and what your career goals were. For real! He never wanted to waste an elevator ride. If you found yourself in the elevator with him — which was actually pretty common — you had a great opportunity to either really impress him, or totally flop.

Even if you don't work in a place where the CEO is just waiting to ask these questions of you, it's a really good idea to have your responsibilities and aspirations summed up in your mind. You never know when you're going to meet someone who could really make a difference in your career, and you want to be prepared for if and when that moment comes.

**Define your objectives.**
Who do you want to be? Streamline your goals and strategies to get you there. Be specific and take measurable steps to create your ideal brand story.

# Developing your Brand

## STEP 1: IDENTIFY YOUR BRAND

*Remember, your brand is a reflection of who you are as a person and a professional. It is the story you tell the world about who you are, what you do, and how you handle yourself. Make a list of all the traits you want to portray to the world. How do you want to be seen?*

_____    _____

_____    _____

_____    _____

## STEP 2: IMRPOVE AND MAINTAIN YOUR BRAND

*In order to improve your brand, make sure you have and continue to do the following.*

1. Google your name and see what comes up and change anything that comes up that does not align with your brand.
2. Clean up your social media. Make sure everything you post aligns with how you want those in the business sector to perceive you.
3. Purchase clothes that match the image you want to portray.

4. Craft a resume that helps sell you, clearly telling your story.

   • To learn how to write an effective resume that helps sell you, sign up for this course on Udemy: *Writing the Resume: Get your Foot in the Door* by Katie Chambers. To receive a 40% discount, making the course only $15.00, enter the following coupon code: KEN_CLIENT. Or just go to this link: https://www.udemy.com/ tutorwithkatie-resumewritingcourse/ ?couponCode=KEN_CLIENT

5. Obtain credentials/certifications and soft skills that will help sell your brand.

6. Align yourself with likeminded people who are headed the same direction you are.

7. Keep a record of all of your successes and unique accomplishments.

8. Look for ways to volunteer in your community.

9. Contribute to the conversation in the workplace, letting your voice and brand be known.

10. Craft your elevator pitch.

11. Streamline all your goals and strategies to help bolster your brand.

# CHAPTER 9

———— ~ ————

# INVEST IN A SUCCESSFUL CAREER AND FUTURE

Don't be afraid to invest in yourself. Many mistakenly believe that millennials want reward without putting in the hard work. I have really found that to be untrue. However, while I wholeheartedly believe millennials do have a desire to work, there is some confusion about what it takes to set oneself up for success. A big part of that is investing in yourself.

People often cite circumstances and resources as the obstacles standing between them and their success. While both of those things are real, I think sometimes they're used as an excuse. Behind every success story, there is struggle — struggle to find the time, struggle to find the resources. That struggle is what's going to prepare you for the future. Purposeful investment — figuring out what investments are worth it and finding ways to pour the time and resources you need into those investments — is what is ultimately going to breed success for you.

Steve Jobs didn't wake up one morning CEO of Apple. He poured enormous amounts of energy and ingenuity into his idea, exercised patience, and then realized his success. People like Steve Jobs don't buy into giving yourself a break by believing excuses. Excuses such as:

**I don't have enough time.**
You do have enough time. It's true that time is finite, but you can rearrange how you spend –time — even if it's temporary — to invest in your career. Maybe because you take this on, it means you don't have enough time for something else (Netflix?). Find the time. Time-management skills are at the crux of developing a successful career, and they are easier to master than you think. Get into a routine, eliminate productivity suckers, and map out each and every day.

**I don't have enough money.**
If you know where to look, there are actually a lot of resources out there to pull from. Common sources include grants, scholarships, private donations, crowdsurfing platforms, and loans. While you are plotting how to obtain funds, continue hammering out the details of your plan, strategies, and goals. A succinct vision will only help show potential lenders that you're serious about securing funds.

**I don't have what it takes.**
If there is a will, there is *always* a way; the only thing stopping it is you. Find your why and let it motivate you to push forward every single day.

**I don't have the skill set.**
Maybe not yet! Part of investing in your career is seeking out skill sets that are going to benefit your career and finding the resources necessary to obtain those skills.

**I don't know where to begin.**
Starting any endeavor can be stressful, especially before you map it out. The best way to get yourself on the road toward success is to plan the steps you're going to take to get there. Sit down and sketch out what you want to accomplish and then work backwards so that you can clearly see the steps you need to take to get there. It's almost

never as overwhelming as you thought once you put pen to paper and map it out.

## Why Self-Investment is Important

You have aspirations for your career — a picture of what you want for your future. Investing in yourself is the best (and only) way to get there. Remember: you are the CEO of the 'company' that is your career. That means that you should put the time and resources into making that brand top notch.

The idea of self-investment may cause you to pause. You may assume that in order to invest in your career, you have to put up a ton of cash up front. There are worthy opportunities to spend money in the self-investment game — workshops, certifications, etc. — but there are also a ton of small investments that you can make that will make a huge impact on your career. Learning how to manage your time, creating a vision for your career, honing your soft skills — these are small adjustments that you can make on a small, day to day level that will have huge impact on your long term job security and success.

When I first transitioned from a corporate job to working as a consultant, my contract got renewed, and I let myself feel really comfortable. I didn't update my resume; I didn't invest in any new skills. I was getting paid, and I wasn't saving nor was I investing in myself. I should have been dedicating a portion of my earnings into building my career, so that I could rise to higher positions and ultimately higher earnings. Not to mention that before long, many of my contracts ended and were not renewed. Without an updated and shining resume, I fell behind my peers, who had been investing in themselves all along — often using company resources to do it.

So I found myself standing there with no contracts and with less skills than my peers. I had the opportunity to take a class costing $1500 that would bring me up to speed with my peers, but I only had two grand in my bank account. Guess what? I made the plunge anyway. I took that class, leaving myself only $500. I knew that it was an important investment and that I needed to go for it, and so I did.

Now, I'm not advocating that everyone go out and spend their last dollars. Instead, I am encouraging you to invest as you go — in small and big ways — so you don't find yourself standing alone in an open field wondering how you can build your skills with limited resources.

Jim Rohn,entrepreneur, author, and motivational speaker, once said, *"formal education will make you a living; self-education will make you a fortune."* This isn't to damper the achievement of a formal education, but what he's implying is that the hallmark of true fortune — true success and happiness — will come from the investments you make in yourself.

## Luck is Where Preparation Meets Opportunity

The term "luck" is used loosely in America. You may think that opportunity falls out of the sky and onto some people's laps. The truth is, "luck" occurs when the right person — bolstered with the right set of circumstance around them — encounters a particular opportunity and is able to seize it. Believing in any other form of luck runs you the danger of cutting yourself way too much slack.

In one of my first corporate jobs, a position was available and one guy got it over a friend of mine. I turned to my friend and said, "Man. You should have gotten that position. He's so lucky." Later that day, my manager and I were in the break room together. He had overheard my comment to my friend, and he pulled me aside and asked me why I figured that guy was lucky. Intimidated, I fumbled my words and came up with something. He listened to what I had to say, but then he paused and said that from the outside it might have looked like that guy got that position easily, but the truth was that he had inquired about that position before it even became available. For the year leading up to the promotion, he spent time taking classes, earning certifications, and shadowing others so that he could be prepared for that job when it became available. At the same time, he stayed 100% on top of his current position, always turning in projects on time or ahead of schedule. He made himself the best he could be so that when that position because available, he was aligned to transition into it with ease.

My buddy, on the other hand, was quietly doing what was asked of him — and nothing more — and secretly hoping he'd get that promotion. But he didn't take the initiative to talk to anyone about it, and he didn't make sure that he was investing the time and resources into himself so that he was the best person for the job once the job became available. Clearly, it wasn't a case of luck — it was a case of one guy knowing what he wanted, while another knew what he wanted *and* was taking the actionable steps necessary to get there.

That experience made me realize I had missed out on opportunities because I wasn't prepared. All of the things I could have done if I could have said — hey, I'm here, and I'm prepared for what you need. It really made me take pause when looking at my future. It helped me see that you need to know what you want way before you expect to get it, and you really have to plot a map to get there.

## Ways to Invest in Yourself

So — how do you invest in yourself? Self-investments can take many forms and can come from many places. For any investment you think you might take on, though, remember to do your homework. Vet the resources you're tapping into: mentors, educational institutions, or workshops. Make sure that your investments are *smart* investments. And remember — the best investment doesn't necessarily mean the highest cost. It means finding the opportunities that have the best accolades. Every time I go to sign up for a speaking engagement or a conference, I do the research to make sure that the conference I'm going to has solid reviews and that the speaker has solid background experience. Always make sure you're investing wisely.

**Find a mentor**.
As discussed, mentors are awesome banks of information and resources. Your soon-to-be-mentor likely took the time to self-invest leading to his or her current position. Therefore, your mentor knows things now that he or she didn't know before. You, now, will know these secrets and tips earlier on than many who went before you.

**Use community resources.**
Maybe you are a bit rusty at speaking in front of groups, or maybe you need some enhancement of your soft skills. Look in the community and figure out ways that you can enhance those skills by becoming more involved. Maybe you can teach a class, which will put you in front of a crowd and help you manage your nerves. Or you could volunteer, helping you to flex that soft skill's muscle.

**Get educated.**
At many career crossroads, it makes sense to invest time and money needed to get an advanced degree, to get a certification, or to attend a conference or a workshop to enhance your skills.

Education can take many forms — higher education degrees, certifications, skill classes, and more — and it'll rarely steer you wrong. If you do intend to get into higher education for an advanced degree —

MFA, PhD, etc. — it's important that you really think it through first. Make sure you understand the cost benefit analysis — will you earn enough with the degree than without to make the degree worthwhile? Also, earning a degree is no small feat. Make sure that you're earning it in the field you really want to work in. Don't just chase it because you don't know what else to do.

**Increase your knowledge.**

Yes, getting a higher education will increase your knowledge, but there are many other ways to grow your brain bank. Seek out people in your *industry community* that make an impression on you; buy their books, their vlogs, and their podcasts; and attend conferences where they may be present. Learn from those who have come before you, cultivate relationships, and never stop learning.

So go on, invest in your skills, your talents, your strengths, your habits, and your brand. Read a book, learn a language, go to a leadership conference, join a club, take a class, take a break, design a personal website, whatever it –is — do something that is going to encourage personal and professional growth. The thing about self-investments is they only depreciate if you let them.

Even if your current company doesn't appreciate your increasing value, someone else will. Once you begin investing in yourself, you no longer focus solely on job security, and you now have the human capital necessary to move freely through corporate America to find an organization which aligns with your goals and appreciates your value, and won't let you go because of it.

## Self-Investment

*Self-investment is ongoing. Make sure you are repeating each of these ways to invest in yourself.*

1. Commit your why statement to memory and let it guide you
2. Map out your career vision every 3 years, making clear goals and creating action steps
3. Create SMART goals aligned with your plans and strategies
4. Plan your day to make sure you are prioritizing and using your time well
5. Evaluate your soft skills and work on improving your weak areas
6. Utilize company resources to build your repertoire of knowledge and skills
7. Find and work with a mentor
8. Improve and maintain your brand, your image

9. Obtain the needed degrees and certifications
10. Attend workshops, conferences, classes that help you improve
11. Read self-help books
12. Meet and associate with like-minded people
13. Find ways to be involved in your community
14. Work on finding and maintaining your work/life balance

# CHAPTER 10

―――――――∽――――――――

# HARD WORK PAYS OFF — IF YOU LET IT

The phrase "Work/Life Balance" first cropped up in the 80's, and it was originally used by recruiters who were trying to lure people into the corporate world while assuring them that they would have a balanced, happy life despite their all-encompassing career. Without any context or realistic expectations built around it though, simply chasing "work life balance" can be a bit like chasing a unicorn. So, let's take a really honest look at what work life balance is and how it can benefit your life and career.

There are a lot of misconceptions when it comes to work/life balance. You may think that when I talk about this concept, I'm proposing that if you work less hours, you'll be happier. That's not necessarily the case. It may not be about working less, but about using the time when you're not at work to indulge in more fulfilling activities. Another misconception is that work/life balance suggests that there should be a 50/50 split — half of your time can be spent working only if half of your time is spent living. This is not necessarily realistic, so if you put all of your eggs in this basket, you are bound to be disappointed and stressed.

Rather than saying "I need to work less" or "I have to have a 50/50 split," you need to take a holistic view of your work and of your life outside of work, and figure out what you need to do in order to feel fulfilled in both of those areas. You may not feel fulfilled by your work if you don't dedicate a significant amount of time to it. And fulfillment outside of the workplace is definitely not always about time — sometimes simply allowing yourself a few hours a week to engage in an organized activity you enjoy (a softball game, golfing, a weekly date night with your spouse) will do wonders for your overall feeling of fulfillment.

So going into this chapter, I think it's really important to establish that I'm not necessarily talking about time, here. I'm talking about quality. I'm talking about mindfulness around the things you want to accomplish in both of these sectors and how you can manage each to respect the other. And this isn't always week to week. Maybe one week you need to travel out of town to go to an event for a client, and you'll be there for a week or so. That week, you probably won't get to engage in all of the home life things that ultimately make you feel fulfilled. But you may be able to then take a little extra time in the following weeks to do more of the things you love to do with your friends and family. In order to feel fulfilled long term, you need to learn to be fluid and flexible in what you expect from both sides your life and what that give and take between them might look like.

Not only is there fluidity in how you achieve balance, but also, the shape that balance takes is going to be different for everyone, and it's probably going to change for you at different points in your life and career. Maybe as you're striving for a promotion, you need to mindfully dedicate more of yourself to work than you do to your family — or maybe at a particular stage in your kids' upbringing, you will make the purposeful decision that you're going to plateau in your career a bit so that you can dedicate more time to home life. It's going to be different for everyone, and there are going to be ebbs and flows.

Why is talking about this necessary? It's no secret that it can be really easy for the young professional to get so sucked into work and striving for success that things like family relationships, leisure time, friendships, and hobbies get ignored. And let me be clear that this is something nearly *everyone* struggles with. Social media posts may not reflect it, but there is hardly anyone out there living a perfectly easily balanced life without stressing over it. That's why you need to pay attention to this and develop a clear plan on how you will achieve this balance. This is a goal for all of us, and it's going to take action to achieve it.

What happens when you don't take the action you need to take to plan for a good work life balance? You burn out. You reach breaking points that usually involve some fury toward your career, which you may blame for the way you're feeling (of course, it's not the job's fault you aren't going to golf every Saturday — it's a lack of clarity around how you're dividing your time). Burnout can break you, and it can throw you way off of your track. Focusing on your work life balance — and what it means —

now can be thought of as preventative medicine. Keep yourself from getting to the point where something needs to give.

## I Burned Out

When I first entered the corporate world, my team was working seventy hour weeks. I didn't even think to complain about that. I was hell-bent on proving myself so I could climb that corporate ladder. I was on a salary, which means I wasn't earning any more money for my seventy hours than I would have for forty. But I was sure that working that hard was going to bring me some benefit somehow, and so I did it.

Two things happened. The first is that I was 100% sucked into my work life. The stress of work was literally all I experienced in my waking hours. That type of never-ending concentrated anxiety has major potential to wreak havoc on one's mental state. The second thing that happened was that I totally neglected all of the things that typically brought me joy. My hobbies went out the window. My relationships weren't being nurtured. It was like I was running toward some unseen goal, and in the wake of my path, these sources of joy from my former life were dying.

This was a recipe for disaster. Being at work too much was adding more negative energy to my soul than it was used to, and neglecting the things that made me happy meant that less positive energy was reaching me than I was used to. The darkness was bound to win.

I didn't have the confidence to say *I'm being overworked*. I didn't know to take care of myself. I thought that ambition would trump all things. I had the illusion that if I put more time in, I'd get to where I was going faster. But in reality, I pushed myself too much, and I burnt out, which ultimately held me back because it warped my relationship toward my life and my work. My relationships were failing. I was growing distant from my family. Relationships take work! You have to connect with people and spend time with them in order for relationships to be maintained and survived. That's something that I wasn't able to do because I was working too much, and I ultimately missed out on some important relationships — some of them forever.

All the while, a lack of recharging time meant that work was grinding my soul until I finally broke. I wanted to walk away completely. Luckily, I realized that instead of leaving altogether, I needed to change something about the way I was handling my work so that my life wasn't taking a complete backseat. I needed to find a work/life balance that would work for me in both my work and in my life.

## Types of Burnouts

A study by the Association for Psychological Science shows that there are typically three different types of burnout:

1. *Overload*
2. *Boredom*
3. *Worn-out*

Each of these comes with a different set of coping mechanisms and a different set of reasons someone goes over the edge.

**Overload.**
People who work so hard to achieve success without striking that healthy work/life balance often hit *overload* burnout, and they rely heavily on emotional venting about the stressors in life. They may say things like, "The company is keeping me down," or "X, Y and Z are keeping me from being as successful." By focusing so acutely on all of the outside forces that are "making" the individual's life the way it is, he or she basically piles on the stress until eventually reaching a point where he or she cracks.

**Boredom.**

The next burnout is common in people who are just plain *bored*. Their jobs offer them no sense of personal development, so they grow cynical and unproductive because they lack stimulation to the degree that they just depersonalize and create as much distance as possible between them and their job. This kind of slow-to-build burnout often results when people do not find out their why, do not plan out their goals, and do not take the time to invest in themselves to grow towards their lifelong dreams.

**Worn Out.**

This type of burnout stems from people's inability to persevere through difficult circumstances while in pursuit of a goal. They experience stress so thoroughly and lack the skills to cope with it so seriously that when the going gets tough, they get overwhelmed and bolt.

Do any of these sound like you? Here are a few more symptoms to look out for.

# Warning Signs

Burnout creeps up on you, it's not a wake-up-one-day-with-it kind of thing; it's a slow roll down the rabbit hole. If you find yourself feeling different from your usual, normal, productive self, maybe it's time to take a much needed mental health break.

**Impaired concentration/forgetfulness.**
You will experience it from time to time, but when you're seriously overworked, this trait may become a bit more prevalent.

**Insomnia/Fatigue.**
Do you lay awake at night thinking of your never-ending to-do list? Insomnia can be the bane of your existence. It slows you down and trips you up. Pay attention if it rears its ugly head.

**Detachment.**
Feeling detached is another tell-tale sign of a looming burnout. One too many calls into work for being sick, showing up late, or taking on more isolated activities and withdrawing into yourself are all danger signs. If you don't usually emotionally distance yourself from work, take pause if you start to feel detached. It may mean you need to reevaluate the balance in your life.

**Depression/Anxiety.**
If you feel yourself being drawn into bouts of depression or anxiety, something needs to shift. You shouldn't be in anguish because of your work. If you find yourself battling these two, reevaluate your work/life balance and think about speaking to a

counselor. Many big companies even offer coaching and counseling opportunities to employees, which may help you strike a better balance.

## Shifting Perspectives

One major step you can take toward balancing your life is to think less about work vs. home and think more about your life as a whole. There was a time in my life when I loved Fridays, and I dreaded Mondays. I saw work as the enemy that was keeping me away from my "real" life. If you are dedicated to being a successful professional, work is your real life. Can you also be dedicated to being a good partner, a good parent, a good friend? Yes, absolutely. That's also part of your real life. These two things don't have to be at odds with one – another — they can be part of the same bigger picture. Days when you are working are not days being spent away from reality — they're days that are contributing to one part of your whole reality. Shifting your perspective in this way can do wonders for helping you feel more balanced and ultimately fulfilled.

Other things you might be able to do to help yourself achieve all that you want in both your life and your career might include:

**Create healthy boundaries.**

Be aware of what it is you want to accomplish and where you need to be (and when) to make that happen. If you're committed to attending your mom's birthday dinner because it's important, then set a wall up around that commitment. If someone asks you to take on some extra work that will keep you from it, turn that project down and be okay with the fact that you're dedicating that time to your mom.

**Use your vacation days.**

Vacation days are meant to be used to recharge. In a work versus life mentality, they are seen as time to "live your real –life"— aka your life without work. This doesn't support a holistic approach to your life. But that doesn't mean that vacation is invaluable. You dedicate a lot of time to work where you put up blinders to your home life. You can do the same for your home life without disregarding the importance of work. Plus, vacation time gives you an opportunity to get intimately in touch with the people and activities that make you feel most alive, which can help to inform your plans for your work/life balance once vacation is over.

**Detach and unplug.**

Everyone is so plugged in these days. Even when you're in bed, you can look at your phone. When you're feeling overwhelmed by anything — work or home — you should turn off the electronics and just sit with yourself; this can do wonders for your mental space.

**Integrate downtime into your daily schedule.**
Create a daily downtime ritual and do your best to stick to it. Hold yourself accountable by putting an X through every day on a wall calendar that you take *ten minutes* to just **be**. The perfectionist in you will want to see that X on every day of the week motivating you to do it, even if it's for the wrong reasons.

Taking time away from your life's work to establish and nurture relationships, find relaxation and enjoy recreation will be the golden ticket to becoming the most successful - and happy - you.

## The Twenty Minute Plan

In addition to the tips above, I've created a technique for myself that really helps me maintain a healthy work/life balance relationship. This is largely about infusing your day with things that bolster the – self — these individuals who exists in both your work life and your home life.

The trick here is to spend five minute each day on the following. It's four parts, so this will take up twenty minutes of your day total. Those twenty minutes can have a huge impact on the other 23 hours and 40 minutes!

**Five minutes for meditation.**
This exercise at the beginning of each day is crucial. Meditating can mean the difference between attacking your day with ferocity and approaching it with an aura of calmness. Meditation centers your mind and calms your spirit. It also helps relieve any tension you feel about the day ahead. Meditation can help you focus on your inner power and remind you that you're important to others.

**Five minutes for planning.**
Once you've meditated, it's time to review the plan for your day that you created the night before. Planning means organizing your tasks so you can be productive without abusing yourself. Prioritize your tasks based on their importance. Try your best to stick to the plan for the day. Having a clear plan for what you want to accomplish helps to keep you focused and stress-free.

**Five minutes for checking in.**
Whether you do it all at once or in one-minute intervals, check up on yourself. Assess how well

you've been able to stick to your plan. Have you accomplished your important tasks? Have you been able to manage your day without losing your cool? There may be times when you'll have to readjust your list of tasks. There are bound to be unforeseen circumstances. But what's important is that you take them in stride.

Avoid letting unexpected events throw your plan out completely. Take a moment to change your approach. Learn how to go with the flow.

**Five minutes for winding down.**
Now that you've come to the end of the day, it's time to wind down. You've probably never allowed yourself the opportunity to do that before. Taking time to wind down is the best way to relieve the stress of the day.

Engage in some relaxing activities. Do you like yoga or would you prefer to sit quietly and listen to jazz music? Let go of what happened today and get ready for tomorrow.

Winding down also opens you up to spending quality time with loved ones. You'll probably agree that at the end of a busy day, you may be too tired to interact with anyone. That will change when you allow yourself to wind down each day.

Once you try it, you'll realize that this approach works. Designating these 20 minutes each day can help you maintain a balance between your professional and personal lives. It can also help you manage all other aspects of your life with relative ease. And you'll enjoy a calmer existence that you didn't think was possible

## Twenty Minute Plan

*Make a copy of this handout and place it in a prominent place in your home and office.*

Morning: Spend 5 minutes meditation

Morning: Spend 5 minutes reviewing your to-to list that you made the night before. Organize and prioritize these tasks, planning out when and how long you will spend on each task.

Throughout the day: Check in and assess how well you have stuck to your plan and make any adjustments if needed.

Evening: Spend 5 minutes winding down. Engage in some relaxing activity.

# CHAPTER 11

---～---

# SHIFTS IN CORPORATE AMERICA

Throughout this text, I've covered a lot. Are you ready? Are you feeling excited about your life and career and all that you can accomplish in it? I hope so! To recap, here's what you're going to be focusing on as you transition from reading to doing:

**Knowing your why.**
This is going to set you up for your end result. You have to have that why factor — you have to know why you're doing what you're doing. If you don't, it's really, really easy to get lost. I've gotten lost myself plenty of times. Always hanging on to that why is a good thing.

**Career vision.**
It's so important to work your vision backwards so you can see every step. Robert Collier, a motivational author, has this quote that I love — "Imagination gives you the picture. Vision gives you the impulse to make the picture your own." Imagination and vision are two different things, but you need both to get to your goal. You have to imagine the career and life you want, one that you find fulfilling and rewarding. Once you have that imagination along with your why, you have to be able to create that vision. That vision is how you get there.

**Strategies, plans, and setting goals.**
Having a foundation in how to set goals and attain those goals is integral to success in any pursuit. Working on goals and strategies to meet those goals is what's going to get you to your vision.

**Time management.**
People don't always realize that time is finite. Time management often takes strategy and practice. In order to get the tasks accomplished that you need to do and indulge in the things you love, you must learn how to allot your time. As you learn to manage your time, you will always need to check in with yourself periodically to make sure you don't get too

comfortable and start to lag on your time management strategies.

**Developing soft skills.**

Soft skills have been in the root of this country since its beginning. Being accepted in multiple circles is a human desire, and it's a skill we have all been working on since day one. With this, you must learn to be adaptable in the work place and beyond. It helps you ease into a new workplace; it helps you develop relationships with clients; and it makes you an overall more employable person.

**Increasing your value — taking advantage of company resources.**

Don't overlook the free gold that's out there for you! Take the time to take advantage of the self-improvement benefits that a company offers. The skills you acquire in additional training are things you can take with you job to job, and often they don't cost you anything other than time. This is one of the best and most overlooked benefits that companies offer — don't waste it!

**Seeking mentorship.**

A mentor is a key that unlocks doors. Look for people who are three to five years ahead of where you and are and who remember what it took to get to where they are now. Mentors are an incredible resource that can help you define the steps you need to take to achieve your goals. They can also keep you on your toes by providing accountability for you.

## Career branding.

As technology evolves, the rules are changing. Before technology, a career brand may have been limited to putting one's best foot forward in the workplace. Today, you have to be aware of the full picture you project of yourself both in and out of the workplace. This goes beyond social media, though that plays a role. You also need to be fully aware of the picture you paint in the workplace. Are you dressed appropriately? Are your soft skills at work helping you interact with superiors, coworkers, and clients in an appropriate manner? Are you dependable? Do you give the impression that you're ambitious? All of this contributes to your overall brand. You can still be your individual you — you don't have to become a corporate robot. You just have to play by — and thrive within — the rules.

## Self-Investment.

Invest in yourself! How can you ever get to any of the places that you've envisioned if you're not willing to invest in yourself? In this chapter, I talked about attending various workshops and obtaining certificates to increase your value. Everything else that I've talked about in this book factors into self-investment, too. Additional knowledge and skills are always going to help you stand out among the crowd. Sacrifice — time, sweat, money — is part of the road to success. Making investments, making plans, making strategies — it's all necessary.

**Enjoy life.**
Someone recently asked me if I get more joy from my personal or my business life. I told this person that I get gratification from both. I'm now at a comfortable place in my personal life because of what I've done throughout my career. I've earned enough money to where some of the anxieties I had when I was younger — mainly, can I pay the bills? — have absolved. I'm not worrying about those things, which means that when I'm home, I can enjoy myself to a greater degree.

# Shifts in Corporate America

So, I've covered a lot. And as I prepare to wrap up, I think it's really important that I touch on the shifts and expansions in corporate America. As corporate America changes, you need to be prepared to take all of the concepts you've mastered in this book and use them to shift and expand right along with the corporate world.

Studies show that 35% of millennials do some form of freelance work. That figure is really high — higher than any generation before us. I first experienced contract work when I was on the road as a consultant. I was working for a corporation, but I started to meet so many people who were independent contractors, which meant that they were getting the consulting contract without a third-party managing the relationship. Over time, I noticed a shift in the amount of people doing similar work for a corporation versus the number of people who were doing it on their own. The independent contractor sector was growing, and they were earning more than those of us who were working in the corporate field.

There was a time when contract work was relegated to tech industries, but millennials have pushed the envelope in terms of what types of work they can be contracted to do. There are people who provide social media expertise via contracts. Marketing experts, receptionists, security, HR, payrolls and billing — so many of the jobs that were once considered in-house and part of the corporation are now independent contractors. Many of these people are able to work remotely and provide their services virtually. The days of needing to be in an office every day are fading — slowly, but they're fading.

Why is this happening? Technology has made the world smaller. And as a result, companies are getting smaller. You don't need as many people physically present on a day to day basis to ensure that a company's operations run smoothly. Companies are finding out faster and more efficient ways to do things — but they're also finding ways to save money. Why have you come into the office to use their office supplies, paper cups, coffee, etc. when they could have you work from home? And then once they have people working from home, they start to think — why pay for benefits when we can just pay these people more day to day and let them decide what to do with the money? This can be beneficial to the contractor, big time. If you have a skill set that is particularly attractive to companies, you can potentially make more money than you would if you were working for a company full time.

Everything we've talked about here — time management, soft skills, career branding, finding a mentor — all of that stuff becomes ten times more important if you're a contractor than if you are trying to work your way up the corporate ladder. When you're an independent contractor, you, yourself, literally become the selling point to working with you. You don't have the bubble of a corporation's reputation to vouch for your skills — you only have yourself and your accolades. In the consulting world, contracts typically last about six months. You need to readily prove your worth in order to get that contract renewed. There is literally no time to dawdle or to let yourself become complacent. You are a walking brand, and if you misrepresent yourself, you run the risk of that contract going to a different individual.

As an independent contractor, your viability at a company is directly linked to your ability to play by the rules. Having someone teach you what those rules are and how you can succeed in that field is undoubtedly going to set you up for a higher success rate than those who don't have someone in their corner. Self-investment is what will separate you from the hundreds of other people offering to do the same thing you're doing. And of course, building your brand is of upmost importance. You need to build a reputation and be known for it.

In the type of environment we have today, though, you have to be on your game even if you are settled into the more 'traditional' corporate path. You have to be 100% dedicated to your brand at all times — if you start to falter, you could easily be replaced, possibly by an independent contractor.

There are obviously some benefits that independent contractors don't get to take advantage of. Having the company pay for schooling in exchange for loyalty, for example. 401k contributions. Profit sharing. Depending on what your goals are, you may want to work for a corporation in order to take advantage of these various benefits

When we look at the changing landscape of the corporate world, it's important that you learn to roll with the changes and not let those skills you've perfected falter as you are adjusting to new realities.

For myself, I've been a student of perfecting my soft skills since I first got a job at fifteen. At fifteen, I shouldn't have even had a job. I made a photocopy of my birth certificate, I whited out the date on the photocopy, typed in a new date that made me a year older than I really was, and photocopied it again. I brought that copy to McDonald's and told them it was a copy of my original birth certificate. They believed me and put me to work. There was a guy there named Stanley who had his soft skills down. He could charm any and all customers — it didn't matter what type of day they had on their back when they walked in, he lifted the weight and inspired them to relax and smile. I saw what he was capable of, and I knew I wanted to have skills like that myself. Thus, I started studying what he was doing, and he actively taught me a thing or two about soft skills.

As I've explained in earlier parts of the book, I had other mentors along the way who made sure I understood soft skills and how they were going to impact my journey. For me, it didn't matter if I was working the register at McDonald's in my old neighborhood or landing a major contract as a consultant — I was focused in the same way on making those skills work for me.

As corporate culture, corporate benefits, and the way that the professional fits into the corporate world grows and shifts, millennials need to remain as focused on themselves and their careers as they were at their first internship, way back when.

In addition to keeping your soft skills at the forefront of your mind across various positions you will hold, you also need to be adaptable within any job where you work as a consultant. As a consultant, you may go from city to city. One week you could be in Los Angeles, CA, and the next week you could be in Binghamton, NY. Those are two cities with vastly different cultures, and you need to be able to fit into them with ease so that you can hit the ground running with your work.

In my own experience transitioning between cultures within the US, people skills — the ones I learned way back when I worked at McDonalds — are just as important now as they were then. I need to be able to look at someone and figure out — quickly — how to get them to trust me, to engage with me, and to listen to what I have to say.

# In Conclusion

I hope that you've found what I've shared in this book useful. When I was coming up in corporate America, nearly everything I've talked about here was something I didn't know. I had to figure out a lot of these things as I went. And from where I'm standing in my career now, I can see that these concepts are really the core foundations for success in corporate America.

Until now, this information wasn't boiled down the way it is here, nor was it readily available to those who were breaking into their careers. Developing this resource was really important to me because I really believe that if you follow the tools in this book, you will set yourself apart from your competitors. If you take advantage of what you've learned here, it will make a world of difference in your life and career.

I hope that charged with the energy of this book, you're ready to start making changes in your life and career that are going to positively impact your future. Maybe you need to focus on the work in some chapters more than others, or maybe you need to implement everything we've talked about here.

Whatever it is that you need to do, I hope you're ready to do it, and that you're inspired to do it. Enjoy the journey.

# ABOUT THE AUTHOR

⁓

Growing up poor in Kansas City—surrounded by the harsh reality of urban inner-city life—Kenneth Cheadle decided to enter the military. Soon after, wanting something more for himself, he attended college and entered Corporate America. As a first generational career professional in his family, Kenneth struggled to find his way in this new environment. After trudging in the trenches, he found his way and climbed the ladder to success. He planned on writing a story of his life, highlighting his life challenges and perseverance, but after noticing many millennials experiencing the same struggles in their careers, he decided to share the basic insights he learned with others. After working ten years as a health consultant, making six figures, he discovered that chasing money was not as satisfying as chasing happiness, and he started making YouTube videos on finding career satisfaction, which led to him finding a new passion: career coaching. His own victory in the face of diverse challenges serves as the catalyst for guiding his clients through finding empowerment. For the past two years, he has worked full time as a career coach, moving his consultant work to part time. When he isn't pushing himself to be the best in his career, he plays golf or poker to help relieve some stress. He understands the importance of maintaining a work/life balance, and he enjoys spending time with his close-knit family and his wife of two years. He also loves to connect with others, encouraging them to seek greater satisfaction and overcome life's challenges. He hopes everyone learns how to take control of his or her career satisfaction and embrace his or her destiny.

CPSIA information can be obtained
at www.ICGtesting.com
Printed in the USA
FFOW03n1114221017
41402FF